MOUS Word 2000
Quick Study Guide

Gini Courter
Annette Marquis
Karla Browning

San Francisco • Paris • Düsseldorf • Soest • London

Associate Publisher: Amy Romanoff
Contracts and Licensing Manager: Kristine O'Callaghan
Acquisitions & Developmental Editor: Sherry Bonelli
Editor and Project Team Leader: Kari Brooks
Technical Editor: Scott Warmbrand
Book Designer and Electronic Publishing Specialist: Bill Gibson
Proofreader: Andrea Fox
Indexer: Rebecca Plunkett
Cover Designer: Design Site

Screen reproductions produced with Collage Complete.
Collage Complete is a trademark of Inner Media Inc.

To all those pioneering souls who have already become Microsoft Office User Specialists.

Acknowledgements

When Microsoft first introduced the MOUS program, it was uncertain whether the program would take off. Sherry Bonelli, our Developmental and Acquisitions Editor par excellence, saw the exciting potential of this program and made sure Sybex was taking a lead in providing the highest quality books for their readers. Thank you, Sherry, for having faith in the project and recognizing the importance of expanding Sybex's offerings as the program grows.

To Kari Brooks, who worked diligently as our editor and saw the manuscript through the production cycle, and to Scott Warmbrand, who offered his valuable field experience as technical editor—our hats go off to you. We are always amazed at how much better our writing is when our editors have had a crack at it.

Thanks also to Bill Gibson, electronic publishing specialist, for creating the typeset pages, and to Andrea Fox for proofreading every word.

Every Sybex book is the result of a coordinated team effort, and we know there are many members of the team we never even hear about. We hope you feel appreciated too and know that we could not do this with out you.

Contents at a Glance

Table of Contents

Introduction

The Microsoft Word 2000 MOUS Study Guide is designed to prepare you for the Microsoft Office User Specialist exams and, in the process, make you a more knowledgeable Word user. Most Word users use less than 15% of the programs features—they learn what they need to know to accomplish a particular task. Chances are, however, that the methods they use are neither the most efficient, nor the most effective. Hidden in Word's menus and toolbars are an incredible array of tools designed to help you produce every type of document, from a simple letter to a 500-page online manual. Knowing how to delve more deeply into Word's features is what sets a competent user apart from the rest. By the time you finish this book, you will be well equipped to impress your colleagues (and maybe even your employer) with your ability to tackle any project with confidence and skill.

About This Book

This book is a study guide organized around the MOUS objectives published by Microsoft. Appendix A gives you more information about the MOUS exams and what you need to do to prepare. There you'll also find a comprehensive list of MOUS objectives (skill sets and activities) you need to know to pass the MOUS exams. It's a good idea to start by reviewing the objectives for both the Core and Expert exams so you know what you aiming for (visit the Microsoft Certification site http://www.mous.net to get the most current information about the guidelines). This book covers each of the activities listed in the guidelines.

The certification map included with the objectives guides you to the correct page number in this book where each activity is presented. Although every objective is covered somewhere in the book, they are not presented in precise order. As experienced trainers who work with beginning and advanced students on a regular basis, we are confident that you'll find it easier to learn the required skills in the order presented here. After you have finished learning each skill, you can then go back through the list in order and make sure you are comfortable completing each of the required activities.

To prepare for an exam, work through one chapter at a time. At the beginning of each section related to a specific MOUS activity, you'll find an heading with the objective number listed in it, which you can look up in Appendix A.

Not all sections relate to specific objectives. We included some additional topics that we think it is important for you to know even if you will not be tested on them (isn't that just like a teacher!). These topics help to round out your understanding of a specific objective and give you the background you need to move ahead.

Throughout the chapter, you'll find summaries of the steps to accomplishing the tasks described in the previous section. Use summaries to review your knowledge and to practice the steps involved in completing a task.

After each major topic or group of topics, Hands On sections give you a chance to apply what you've learned. If you can complete these exercises *without* help from the book, you should be in pretty good shape for the exam. We've included the objectives the exercises relate to so you can refer to the text if you need assistance.

A Final Check

When you complete an entire chapter, review the objectives once again and see if there are any topics that you are uncertain about. Go back and review those sections in the text and try the Hands On exercises a second time using different documents. If you're still have difficulty, make a note of it and go on to the next topic. Working on related topics sometimes causes the topic with which you're struggling to fall into place.

When you've finished all the topics, you're ready to take the MOUS exam. Do the best you can—you can always take it again if find out the first attempt was only a practice round.

We'd Love to Hear From You!

We've provided you with a variety of tools to help you on your path to certification. We hope that you'll find them useful, challenging, and fun as you improve your Microsoft Office skills. If you'd like to let us know about your experiences with this book and with taking the exams, we'd love to hear from you. Good luck!

Annette Marquis, Gini Courter, and Karla Browning

Sybex, Inc.

1151 Marina Village Parkway

Alameda, CA 94501

e-mail: info@triadconsulting.com

CHAPTER

1

Working in Word 2000

Whether it's your company's annual report or a one-page letter to a client, Word 2000 has the powerful tools you need to create the document. Word is more than just a word processor. It has to be! Business documents require much more than simply typing text that wraps at the margin. Administrators, managers, and staff expect documents to have that "published" look, and Word has all the features to produce professional-looking documents in a snap! Word is just one program in the Microsoft Office 2000 suite that includes 32-bit versions of these applications:

- Word: word processor
- Excel: spreadsheet
- Access: database
- PowerPoint: presentation software
- Outlook: desktop information manager
- Publisher: design and layout software
- FrontPage: Web design and management software
- PhotoDraw: graphics and photo editing tool

These are the latest, most powerful versions of Microsoft's award-winning office productivity tools. There are various editions of Office 2000—Office Standard, for example—and each Office 2000 edition contains different combinations of the applications listed above. But all versions of Office 2000 contain Word, the flagship product of Office 2000. Like all Office 2000 programs, Word 2000's integration features are better than ever before: you'll see improved integration between Word and other applications, between yourself and other users, and between Word and the Web.

The Office 2000 components are amazing tools, and mastering them can be a challenge. But this mastery provides greater opportunities for you to earn the respect of your boss, customers, and co-workers.

Word 2000 is jam-packed with powerful new features. In this chapter, you'll learn to work in the Word application window, and to enter and edit text.

Mastering the Word 2000 Interface

This chapter will familiarize you with basic features of Word 2000, including features you may have used in other Office 2000 applications. If you're experienced with Office 95 or Office 97 programs, a lot of this will be old territory, but you should still work through this chapter, particularly if you're used to word processing in programs written for Windows 3.1 or the Mac. The 32-bit versions of Windows (Windows 95, Windows 98, and Windows NT, which we'll collectively refer to as Windows throughout this book) and Office 2000 have some subtle time savers, like the ability to manage files in standard dialog boxes. So whatever your prior experience, we recommend you skim this chapter; you're sure to pick up one or two new concepts that you'll use over and over.

Launching Word 2000

With Windows applications, there is usually more than one way to get the job done. You can start Word 2000 in three different ways: click the Word icon on the Office Shortcut bar, use the Start menu to open a New Office Document, or navigate through the Programs menu to the Microsoft Word menu item.

The Microsoft Office Shortcut bar does not automatically appear the first time you use Office 2000. To open it, click the Start button and choose Programs ➤ Microsoft Office Tools ➤ Microsoft Office Shortcut Bar. You'll be asked if you want it to be displayed automatically when you launch Windows, and then the Shortcut bar will appear in its default position along the right side of the screen. You can position the Shortcut bar anywhere you like on your screen: on the left or right, along the top or bottom, or as a free-floating palette of tools.

Simply "grab" the Shortcut bar by clicking and holding on the gray line at the top-left end of the toolbar, position the mouse in the new location, and release the mouse button.

TIP The Word shortcut doesn't appear on the Shortcut bar by default. To add it, click the icon at the beginning (or top) of the bar and choose Customize from the menu. Click the Buttons tab and scroll through the list until you see Microsoft Word. Click the check box in front of Microsoft Word, and any other Office programs you wish to place on the Shortcut bar, then click OK.

The Shortcut bar is the easiest way to launch Word 2000. Simply click the Word icon and the program launches to a blank document ready for your text. If you elect not to show the Shortcut bar on your desktop, try one of these other two ways to open a new document or an Office application. Click the Windows Start button to open the Start menu.

You can easily create new documents from the Windows Start menu. Selecting New Office Document opens the New Office Document dialog box, shown on the next page. Each tab contains *templates* for a number of similar documents. Some of the templates (for example, the Fax templates) include text, graphics, or other content. Blank document templates for all the applications—a blank template for an Access database, Word document, Excel worksheet, and PowerPoint presentation— are found on the General page of the New Office Document dialog box. Choose Blank Document to get started in Word and then click OK. If you prefer to launch Word and then open a document, choose Programs from the Start menu. Select Microsoft Word to launch it.

If you've already launched Word, you have two ways to create a new document. Click the New button on the Standard toolbar to open a new, blank document. If you want a new template instead of a blank document, choose File ➤ New from the *menu bar* to open the New dialog box with Word templates.

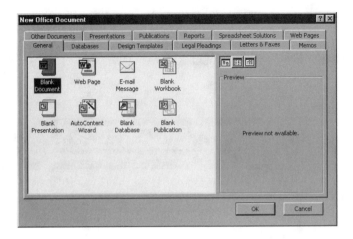

NOTE   See Chapter 3 for more on working with templates.

Using the Word 2000 Application Window

If you're already familiar with the *application window* in Excel or another Office application, getting around in the application window in Word will be a piece of cake. Working in Windows applications is like déjà vu: you'll swear you've seen certain features and tools before. Figure 1.1 shows the Word 2000 application window.

At the top of the Word application window is a *title bar* that contains three buttons: Minimize, Maximize or Restore, and Close. Use these buttons to change the size of your window or to close the window itself. When you're working in Word, you'll usually want to maximize the window. Minimizing Word before you switch to another application frees up system resources, making more memory available to the active application. When a window is maximized, the Restore button is displayed.

When it is restored, the Maximize button is displayed. Even with the Word window maximized, the Windows Taskbar shows all open applications, so you can easily switch between open applications by clicking an application's Taskbar button. Clicking the Close button on the title bar closes the active application, returning you to the Windows desktop or to another open application.

F I G U R E 1.1: Word application window

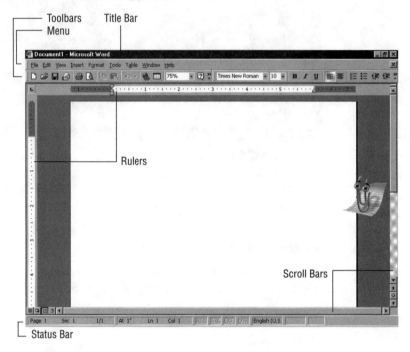

Using Features in the Document Window

In Word, your work area is known as the *document window*. Here you're surrounded by the tools you need to get the job done: *scroll bars* to move the display, a *status bar* to keep you informed of an operation's progress, and the *command bars* at the top of the screen to access all the program's features. You'll use two types of command bars: menu bars and toolbars. The menu bar organizes the features into categories: File, Edit, Help, etc. Clicking on any of the categories opens a list of related features from which you can choose. Many of the menu bar options open dialog boxes that allow you to set several options at once related to the feature you choose—all the print options, all the font settings, and so on.

Toolbars are the command bars with graphical buttons located below the menu bar. Toolbars make many of the most commonly used features only one click away. Use toolbars when you want a shortcut to a common feature and the menu bar when you want to see *all* the options related to a feature. *ScreenTips* provide additional help with commands. If you're uncertain which toolbar button to use, point to the button and hover for a moment; a ScreenTip will appear, showing the button's name.

Word 2000 displays the Standard and Formatting toolbars of previous versions in one row to conserve space in the document window. An option to display frequently used commands is enabled by default, so buttons you use more often are displayed while little-used buttons are moved off the toolbar. If a toolbar button you want to use is not available, click the More Buttons button at the right end of the toolbar and choose the button from the list. It will bump a less frequently used button off your toolbar.

Word 2000 menus also display the features you use most often. If a pull-down menu has more than a handful of commands, less commonly used commands are "folded up." Click the set of small double arrows at the bottom of a pull-down menu to reveal all the menu commands, or wait a few seconds, and the menu will "unfold"—you don't even need to click the mouse.

NOTE   To display full menus and view the complete Standard and Formatting toolbars on separate rows, choose View ➢ Toolbars ➢ Customize and clear the first three check boxes on the Options tab.

Objective W2000.3.4

You probably already know about clicking the arrows at the top and bottom of the vertical scroll bar to scroll up and down in a document. Word 2000 has a number of other tools that make it easy to navigate documents of any length. Rather than using the scroll bar arrows, you can drag the scroll bar's scroll box to display a *ScrollTip* that shows the page number you are scrolling past. (Try reading that sentence three times quickly!) If the document has headings, the heading also appears in the tip.

 Another way to get around in your document is by browsing. On the bottom of the vertical scroll bar is a set of Browse buttons: Previous Page, Select Browse Object, and Next Page.

 Click the Select Browse Object button to open a menu, and then select the object type you'd like to browse.

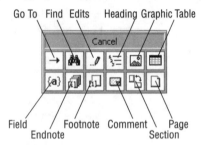

Hover over a button to see a ScreenTip to let you know the type of objects by which you can browse. Select an object type then use the Previous and Next buttons (located directly above and below the Select Browse Object button) to move to the next object of that type in your document.

Objective W2000.3.8

If you want to move forward or backward a specific number of objects (for example, forward ten pages or backward seven pages) choose Go To in the Select Browse Object menu to open the Go To dialog box. Choose the type of object (page) from the Go To What list, and then enter directions in the textbox control: use +10 to move forward ten pages, or −7 to move backward seven pages.

Ways to View Your Document

There are several ways to view documents in Word 2000; the "best" view depends on whether you are outlining, writing, preparing to print, or just reading a document. To the left of the horizontal scroll bar are the View buttons.

 Normal: Used for entering, editing, and basic formatting of text. Headers, footers, graphics, and columns are not visible in this view.

 Web Layout: Word displays your document just as it will appear in a Web browser. Because of the new Web capabilities of Office 2000, a document appears almost exactly the same in Web Layout view and Normal or Print Layout view.

 Print Layout: Allows you to work with your document exactly as it will look when it is printed.

 Outline: Useful when you are developing a document's structure and content, and when you want to create a preliminary outline or review an outline while developing a document.

Entering Text

Few people can type a perfect first draft. There are always major or minor changes to be made once a document is on screen. This section covers basic editing with Word.

The Insertion Point

The insertion point (the screen object formerly known as the cursor) is the flashing vertical bar that indicates where the next character you type will appear. You'll see the blinking insertion point as soon as you open a document.

> You'll notice that the Insertion Point moves as you add text to the page. In Word 2000, you can click and type anywhere on the page, without pressing Tab to move to the right, or pressing Enter to move down.

Just begin typing. Your text will automatically wrap to the next line when you reach the right margin. Within a paragraph, just let text wrap automatically to the next line. Pressing Enter at the end of a line inserts a *hard return* to create a new paragraph or a blank line. To correct mistakes that you make while typing, use the Backspace key to delete characters to the left of the insertion point, or the Delete key to delete to the right of the insertion point.

I

When you move the mouse pointer into an area where you can enter or edit text, the pointer changes to an I-beam. To edit existing text, move the insertion point by moving the I-beam to the text you want to edit. Click, and the insertion point will jump to the new position. Then you can type new text, or delete existing text, at the insertion point.

In Normal view, you will see a black horizontal line at the left margin. This represents the end of your document. In Normal view, you cannot move the insertion point or insert text or objects below the marker until you claim the space by entering text or by pressing the Enter key. Figure 1.2 shows the insertion point and the End of Document marker.

F I G U R E 1.2: Insertion point and End of Document marker

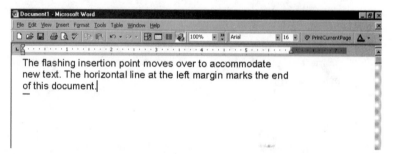

Click and Type

Objective W2000.3.17

In previous versions of Word, you had to "lay claim" to an area of your document before you could use your mouse to position the insertion point there. For example, if you wanted to type some text out near the right margin, you had to press Tab several times to get there. Now, if you're in Print

Layout or Web Layout view, you can double-click anywhere on the page and then type text where you clicked. This new feature of Word 2000 is called Click and Type. Here's how it works:

- If you double-click on the right side of the page, text is right-aligned.
- If you double-click on the left side of the page, text is left-aligned.
- If you double-click in the center of the page, text is centered.

Remember, you can only make use of Click and Type if you're working in Print Layout or Web Layout view.

TIP See "Aligning and Formatting Paragraphs" in Chapter 2 for more information about aligning text.

Behind the Scenes in Word 2000

Word 2000 tries to make your life easier by watching what you're doing and figuring out how it can be most helpful. As you enter text (see Figure 1.3), Word's invisible features are helping you in ways that you'll learn about in more depth later in this chapter and in Chapter 2:

- The Office Assistant evaluates what you are doing to see if it has any suggestions.
- The AutoCorrect feature automatically corrects misspelled words that are in the AutoCorrect list such as *teh* and *adn*.
- The Spelling and Grammar feature reviews your text to determine if there are other possible misspellings or grammatical errors.

F I G U R E 1.3: Office Assistant, Spelling, and Grammar features in action

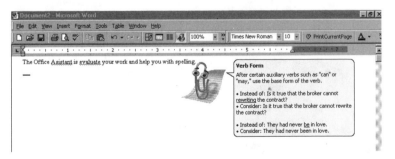

Using the Keyboard to Move the Insertion Point

There are lots of keyboard shortcuts to help you quickly move the insertion point to a new place in your document. You can use the arrow keys to move the cursor up a line, down a line, and one character to the left or right, or you can use the special keys listed in Table 1.1.

T A B L E 1.1: Navigation Keys

Key	Action
Home	The beginning of the current line
End	The end of the current line
Ctrl+Home	The beginning of the document
Ctrl+End	The end of the document
Page Up	Up one screen
Page Down	Down one screen
Ctrl+Page Up	The top of the screen
Ctrl+Page Down	The bottom of the screen
Ctrl+Left Arrow	One word to the left
Ctrl+Right Arrow	One word to the right

Overtype and Insert Modes

▶ *Objective W2000.1.8*

The default editing mode in Word is Insert: if you enter new text in the middle of existing text, the original text will move to the right to accommodate it. If you want to overtype existing text, turn on Overtype mode. To toggle between Insert and Overtype modes, press the Insert key on the keyboard or double-click the control on the status bar labeled OVR. OVR will turn black, indicating that Overtype mode is active:

Hands On

Objectives W2000.3.4, 3.17, and 1.8

1. Start a new Word document. Enter two or three lines of text. Enter a grammatically incorrect sentence (like "People is crazy.") and notice that it is marked with a green line (you may have to press Enter for the green line to appear).

2. Use the shortcut keys listed in Table 1.1 to move around the document. Move the insertion point to the beginning of the document, and use Ctrl+Delete to delete each word in the first sentence.

NOTE   The Word 2000 grammar-checking feature takes advantage of "down-time" to review your completed sentences. If you intentionally make a grammatical error, you may have to move on to the next sentence or next paragraph before it will catch up with you and mark it as questionable.

---

3. Start a new Word document and switch to Print Layout view.

   a) Use Click and Type to center a heading at the top of the page.

   b) Use Click and Type to enter a paragraph of text at the left margin.

   c) Move to the bottom of the page and use Click and Type to enter some text that is right-aligned.

   d) Close the practice document without saving.

Editing Document Text

You can tell that a person is a Word power user because they use very few steps to complete a task. They're not just proficient: they're *efficient*, particularly with skills that are used frequently in Word. Knowing several ways to select and replace text will let you streamline many of the other tasks you'll be doing with your documents.

Quick Ways to Correct Mistakes

Helping you correct mistakes is one of the many things Word 2000 does exceptionally well. In its simplest form, Word will let you erase existing text manually. At its most powerful, Word can automatically correct the words you most commonly misspell.

Backspace and Delete

Most people are familiar with using the Backspace and Delete keys on the keyboard to delete text, but you're not alone if you confuse when to use which one.

- Backspace (the left-pointing arrow above Enter on the keyboard) erases one character to the *left* of the insertion point.

- Delete erases one character to the *right* of the insertion point.

Use whichever is more convenient, based on where your insertion point is.

Undo, Redo, and Repeat

Objective W2000.1.1

Word 2000 is exceptionally forgiving. The Undo button on the Standard toolbar lets you reverse an action or a whole series of actions you have taken. (The Undo button will dim when there is no action you can undo.) Click the drop-down arrow next to the Undo button and scroll down the history to reverse multiple actions in one step.

If you change your mind again, clicking the Redo button reverses the last Undo. In Word 2000, you can use the Undo and Redo histories to reverse multiple actions, all the way back to what was displayed on screen when you started or opened this document. Once you save and exit Word, the Undo and Redo histories are cleared for all documents.

Occasionally, you'll want to repeat your last action. Click Edit ➤ Repeat on the menu. If the Repeat command is unavailable, you haven't completed a repeatable action. You'll also find the Undo and Redo commands on the Edit menu.

Selecting, Moving, and Copying

Whether you are correcting a few mistakes or rearranging your entire document, the first step in any kind of document formatting is selecting text. Once text is selected, it can be moved, copied, deleted, aligned, or formatted.

Selecting Text

You can always drag to select text—even in a dialog box. To select by dragging, move the I-beam to the beginning or the end of the desired text string, hold down the mouse button, and move in the desired direction. Selected text changes to reverse video—the opposite color from text that isn't selected. To unselect text, click anywhere in the document.

WARNING Selected text is automatically deleted if you press any key on the keyboard. If you accidentally delete text in a document, click Undo. Undo won't work in dialog boxes.

Selecting text doesn't have to be a drag; there are a number of other ways to select. You can use any of these methods, but some methods are easier in certain situations. For example, if you've ever used drag to select text over multiple pages, you have already experienced the terrors of an out-of-control accelerated mouse pointer. On the other hand, if you choose another method to select such as Shift-select (see Table 1.2 below), you can select large amounts of text smoothly.

T A B L E 1.2: Selecting Text in Word

To select:	Do this:
A word	Double-click anywhere in the word.
A sentence	Hold Ctrl and click anywhere in the sentence.
A paragraph	Triple-click anywhere in the paragraph, or move the pointer into the left margin so the pointer changes to a right-pointing arrow, then double click.

T A B L E 1.2:   Selecting Text in Word *(continued)*

To select:	Do this:
Single line	Move the pointer into the left margin. When the pointer changes to a right-pointing arrow, point to the desired line and click.
Entire document	Choose Edit ➢ Select All from the menu bar, or hold Ctrl and click in the left margin, or Ctrl+A (keyboard shortcut), or triple click in the left margin.
Multiple lines	Move the pointer to the left margin. With the right-pointing arrow, point to the first desired line and click. Without releasing the mouse button, drag to select additional lines.
Multiple words, lines, or sentences	Move the I-beam into the first word, hold the mouse button, drag to the last word, and release.
Multiple words, lines, or sentences using Shift-select	Click on the first word, and then release the mouse button. Move the I-beam to the last word, hold Shift, and click. Everything between the two clicks is selected.

If you begin entering text when other text is selected, the selected text is deleted and the text you enter will replace it. This is an easy way to replace one word or phrase with another. It also works when you don't want it to—for example, when you forget you still have text selected from a previous action. When you are finished working with selected text, click somewhere in the document to remove the selection.

Moving and Copying Text with Cut, Copy, and Paste

▶ *Objective W2000.1.9*

Now that you can select text, you can move and copy text. When you *move* a selection, the selected text is deleted and placed in the new location. *Copying* text leaves the selected text in place, and creates a copy in the new location.

You move text by cutting it from its current location and pasting it in a new location. When you cut a block of text, it is deleted from your document and copied to the *clipboard*. Copying text moves a copy of the text to the clipboard without deleting the original. The clipboard is part of the computer's memory set aside and managed by Windows. The clipboard can hold only one piece of information at a time, but that piece of information can be text, a graphic, or even a video clip. And as you'll see in "Pasting Multiple Items" on page 19, Office has its own clipboard that can hold up to a dozen items. Moving or copying text is a four-step process: select, cut/copy, move the insertion point, and paste.

Moving and Copying Text

1. Select the text you want to move or copy.

 2. Click the Cut or Copy button on the Standard toolbar

 OR choose Edit ➢ Cut or Edit ➢ Copy from the menu

OR right click within your selected text and choose Cut or Copy from the shortcut menu.

3. Move the insertion point where you want to place the text.

 4. Click the Paste button,

OR choose Edit ➢ Paste from the menu,

OR if you like using the shortcut menu, you can combine steps 3 and 4 by right-clicking where you want to place the text and choosing Paste from the shortcut menu.

All the moving and copying techniques work with pictures or other objects just as they do with text. For more information on working with Word objects, see Chapter 5.

TIP   Cut, Copy, and Paste are standard Windows functions that have corresponding shortcut keys that you can use even if menu and toolbar options are not available. Select the text or object and press Ctrl+X to cut, Ctrl+C to copy, or Ctrl+V to paste.

Copying and Moving Text Using Drag-and-Drop

You'll find it easy to move and copy text short distances using a method called *drag-and-drop*. Drag-and-drop works best when you can see both the *source*, the location of original text, and the *destination*, the place you want the moved or copied text to appear.

Moving Text Using Drag-and-Drop

1. Identify the text you want to move and its destination.

2. Select the text.

3. Drag the text to its new location while holding down the right mouse button. Drop the selection into position by releasing the mouse button.

4. Select Move Here from the shortcut menu.

Use these techniques to move or copy text from one location to another in a single document and move or copy text between documents. If you want to work with more than one document, open both documents, and choose Window ➤ Arrange All to see both documents. (When you want to work on just one of the documents again, click the Maximize button on the document's title bar.)

Copying Text Using Drag-and-Drop

1. Identify the text you want to copy and its destination.

2. Select the text.

3. Drag it to its new location while holding down the right mouse button. Drop the text into position.

4. Select Copy Here from the shortcut menu.

You can also use the left mouse button to drag and drop text, but you don't get the shortcut menu. Instead, the text is moved to the new location with no questions asked. If you want to copy text with the left mouse button, you must hold down the Ctrl key while dropping the text. It's easy to forget to hold down Ctrl or accidentally release Ctrl before the text is dropped, so it is good to get in the habit of dragging with the right mouse button.

Pasting Multiple Items

 A new feature of Office 2000 is Collect and Paste, which lets you copy up to 12 items to a temporary clipboard where you can select and paste them all at once. This makes it easier to move several items from one place to another without forcing you to scroll back and forth through the document.

Cut or copy your items in the order you'll want to paste them in using Edit ➤ Copy or Edit ➤ Cut, and the Clipboard toolbar appears. After you move to the new location in the document where you want to paste the items, paste them one by one from the Office clipboard by clicking each icon and clicking Paste. Choose Paste All to paste the entire contents of the Office clipboard at the insertion point.

WARNING   Collect and Paste is a feature of Office 2000. In non-Office applications, you'll still use the Windows clipboard, which can only hold one item at a time.

Hands On

Objectives W2000.1.1 and 1.9

1. Start a new blank document and type a five-sentence paragraph of sample text.

   a) Select a word, then deselect it.

   b) Select the entire paragraph two separate times. Use two different methods to select a paragraph of text.

2. Select the fourth sentence.

   a) Use Cut and Paste to move the sentence to the beginning of the paragraph.

   b) Select two more sentences and copy each to the clipboard.

   c) Paste each sentence back into your document in the opposite order you copied them. Close this document without saving.

3. Enter two paragraphs of at least three sentences each in a new document. Experiment with the text selection techniques you learned until you feel comfortable using them.

4. Start a new document and enter the following text:

   ```
   This is the third sentence of Doc 1.
   This is the first sentence of Doc 2.
   This is the fourth sentence of Doc 2.
   This is the first sentence of Doc 1.
   ```

5. Save the text as Doc 1.

6. Start another new document and enter the following text:

   ```
   This is the third sentence of Doc 2.
   This is the fourth sentence of Doc 1.
   This is the second sentence of Doc 1.
   This is the second sentence of Doc 2.
   ```

7. Save the text as Doc 2.

8. Using drag-and-drop techniques, rearrange the sentences so they appear in the correct order in the proper document. (With both documents open, choose Window ➢ Arrange All to see both documents at once.)

9. Close both documents without saving changes, and then open them and start again. This time use Cut and Paste to move the sentences. Which method did you prefer?

Working with Files

One of the great things about Office 2000 is that the dialog boxes used for common file functions are similar in all the applications. So if you're familiar with Excel or PowerPoint dialog boxes, you'll have a head start here in Word.

Saving a File

Objective W2000.4.1

 When you're finished working with a document or have completed a sizable amount of work and want to store it before continuing, choose File ➤ Save from the menu bar, or click the Save button on the Standard toolbar to open the Save As dialog box.

The dialog box opens to your default *folder* (directory), but clicking in the Save In text box opens a drop-down list of accessible drives, as shown below. Select a drive, and the folders on the drive are displayed in the pane below the list.

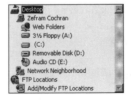

Double-clicking any folder opens it so that you can view the files and folders it contains. When you have located the proper drive and folder, enter a filename in the File Name text box at the bottom of the dialog box. With Word 2000, filenames can be up to 256 characters long, use uppercase and lowercase letters, and contain spaces. They can't contain punctuation other than underscores, hyphens, and exclamation points. And unlike filenames on the Macintosh, they are not case-sensitive: *MY FILE* and *My File* are the same filename. Make sure the name of the current drive or folder appears in the Save In text box, then click the Save button to save the file.

WARNING   All the Office 2000 program dialog boxes locate documents based on file *extension*—the three characters following a period in a filename. For example, Word documents have the .doc extension. Don't create your own extensions or change the extensions of existing documents. If you do, Word will have trouble finding your files—and that means so will you!

Creating a New Folder

Objective W2000.4.4

When you're saving a file, you may decide to create a new folder to house it and other files you'll create later. To create a folder, click File ➤ Save like you normally would to begin the Save process. Use the Save In drop-down list to navigate to the drive or folder within which you want to create the new folder. Click the New Folder button on the toolbar to open a New Folder dialog box. Type the name for the folder (following the same rules as filenames) and press Enter or click OK to create the folder. Then double-click to select the new folder, name your file, and click Save.

Using Save As

Objective W2000.4.3

After you've saved a file once, clicking Save saves the file without opening the Save As dialog box. If you want to save a previously saved file with a new name or save it in another location, choose File ➤ Save As from the menu bar to open the Save As dialog box, where you can specify a new name and/or a different location for the file. The Save As feature is particularly useful if you are using an existing document to create a new document and you want to keep both the original *and* the revised document.

If you share files with people using other programs, or older versions of Word, they may not be able to open your Word 2000 files. You can, however, save your file in a format they can open. In the Save As dialog box, scroll through the Save As Type drop-down list and select an appropriate file format:

Closing a File

To remove a document from the document window, choose File ➤ Close or click the Close button on the right end of the menu bar, directly below the application window's Close button. If you close a document that has been changed since it was last saved, you will be prompted to save your changes.

NOTE   If you have opened more than one document window, you won't see a Close button on the menu bar. Click the Close button on the title bar, and it will close the active document.

Opening an Existing File

Objective W2000.4.2

You don't have to launch Word to open an existing Word 2000 document. If the document was created recently, click the Windows Start button and open the Documents menu. If the document appears there, you're in luck—you can open it directly by selecting it from the menu. Or you may be browsing through your folders in Windows Explorer or My Computer and see a document you want to open. Just double-click the file (or right-click and choose Open from the shortcut menu) to start Word and open the file.

If you have already launched Word, click the File menu and see if the document you want to retrieve appears at the bottom. If so, you can open it by clicking it.

If you're already working in Word and want to open an existing document that doesn't appear at the bottom of the File menu, click the Open button on the Standard toolbar to open the Open dialog box, shown in Figure 1.4.

F I G U R E 1.4: Word Open dialog box

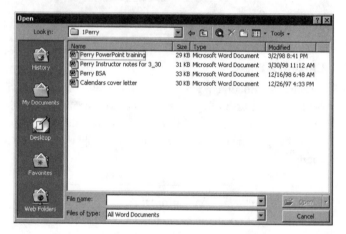

Use the Look In drop-down list to locate the proper folder. When you select a folder to Look In, its files are displayed in the pane below the Look In field. Double-click on a file to open it, or select the file and then click the Open button or press Enter.

Hands On

Objectives W2000.4.1, 4.2, 4.3, and 4.4

1. Start Word and type a short sentence into a blank document.

    a) Save the file in the My Documents folder and name it Practice 1.

    b) Add another sentence to Practice 1. Use the Save As command to name the revised file Practice 2; save it in My Documents.

    c) Close both documents and close Word.

2. Open Practice 2 using the Windows Documents menu.

3. Open Practice 1 using the Open button on the Word toolbar.

4. Close Practice 2, and then add another short sentence to Practice 1. Use Save As to save *Practice 1* in a new folder within My Documents named Practice Docs. If you wish, you can use this new folder to store all the exercises you do in this book.

Print Preview and Printing

Objectives W2000.3.1 and 3.2

 Word allows you to preview a document before printing—good for you, good for your printer, good for the environment. Click the Print Preview button on the Standard toolbar to open the Preview window, shown in Figure 1.5

FIGURE 1.5: Print Preview lets you to see your document before printing it.

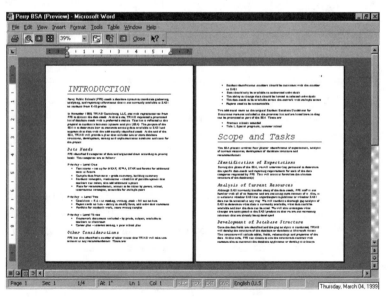

The Preview window has its own toolbar with options for document viewing. Use the toolbar buttons to view one page, multiple pages, full screen, or set a specific zoom percentage. In Print Preview, your mouse pointer shape becomes a magnifier so you can zoom in on different parts of your document with one click. Click again to zoom back out.

When your text runs slightly longer than you wanted it to, you'll want to know about the Shrink to Fit button. This tool works best with short documents (three or fewer pages). If the last page runs over by only a few lines, clicking Shrink to Fit will decrease the font size in the entire document so all the text fits on one fewer page.

NOTE If the last page has a fair amount of text, Word won't be able to shrink it. A message box will appear to let you know that Word can't shrink the text.

You can undo a Shrink to Fit operation by clicking Edit ➤ Undo Shrink to Fit, but do it right away if you don't like the results. After you've saved and closed the document, there is no easy way to undo Shrink to Fit.

If you're ready to print one copy of the entire document on your default printer, click the Print button on the Print Preview toolbar. If you want to return to Word and continue editing, click the Close button on the toolbar.

NOTE The Print button also appears on the Standard toolbar, so you can send documents to the printer without being in Print Preview.

When you want to print anything other than one full copy of the active document using the default printer, choose File ➤ Print from the menu bar to open the Print dialog box. Here you can select a different printer, choose a number of copies, and specify what should be printed. Clicking the Options button at the bottom of the dialog box opens an Options page where you select print quality and other settings.

NOTE Print settings are described in Chapter 2.

Hands On

Objectives W2000.3.1 and 3.2

1. Create a new document or open an existing document.

   a) View the document in Print Preview.

   b) If the document has more than one page, view two pages at once.

   c) Use your mouse to zoom in on a paragraph, then zoom back out.

   d) Print one copy of the document on your default printer.

   e) Close Print Preview.

CHAPTER 2

Mastering the Basics of Word

Whether you are a new or seasoned Word user, Word 2000 has all the features you'll need to create professional-looking documents. Word 2000 is loaded with helpful, timesaving features that allow you to focus on the content of your documents rather than on how to use the software. In this chapter, we'll begin with Word features that are inherited from Office, such as the Office Assistant, Spelling, and Auto-Text. Then you'll learn more editing techniques you can apply to your Word documents, such as how to align paragraphs, create bulleted and numbered lists, navigate complex documents, work with additional language tools, and print files.

Configuring the Office Assistant

Objective W2000.4.9

The *Office Assistant* is Microsoft's social help interface. The Office Assistant crosses all applications and provides help for specific features of each application. You can choose from several Assistants in the Assistant context menu. Each has its own personality: there is Rocky the power puppy; Mother Nature, symbolized as a globe; and an animated Genius with a resemblance to Albert Einstein.

In this version of Office, the Office Assistant lives as a separate object within the application window and displays tips that guide you to better ways to complete a task. The Assistant will offer help the first time you work with a feature or if you have difficulty with a task. Sometimes the offer to help is subtle—Clippit will blink, Rocky will wag his tail, or a lightbulb will appear over the head of the genius. Sometimes the Assistant can be entertaining; for example, the Assistant icon becomes animated during certain basic tasks such as saving or checking spelling. However, some offers of help can be downright intrusive. If, for example, you open a Wizard, the Office Assistant pops up to ask if you'd like help with the feature, even if you've used the Wizard on numerous occasions.

When you need help, simply click the Assistant icon to activate it, and open a search window. Then type a word or phrase that describes what you need help on ("Change text size," for example) and click Search. The Office Assistant will display a list of topics related to the word or phrase you typed. Choose one of those topics by clicking the blue button preceding it. You'll see a Microsoft Word Help window open displaying steps to follow to complete the task you chose from the list of topics. Close the Help window when you're through. Click anywhere in your document to proceed.

After you've worked with Word 2000 for a few days, you might decide that you'd like a little less help from the Assistant. To change the Assistant's options, right-click the Assistant and then choose Options from the shortcut menu to open the Office Assistant dialog box. Click the Options tab to display the Options page, shown in Figure 2.1.

F I G U R E 2.1: Office Assistant dialog box

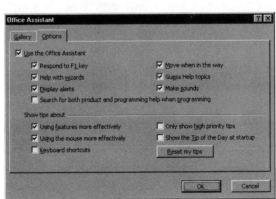

All the Office 2000 programs share the Assistant, so you can't use a different Assistant in each Office application. Any options you change here in Word affect the Assistant in all the Office programs. Therefore, if you set a decreased level of assistance with Word, you'll get the same decreased level of assistance with Excel.

When you're ready to go it alone, you can right-click the Assistant and choose Hide from the shortcut menu to return it to the Standard toolbar. If you start to get lonely, just click the Office Assistant button to invite the Assistant back into your office.

TIP For help with any dialog box in Word 2000, click the dialog box Help button (the question mark), then click on the dialog box control you want help with.

Hands On

Objective W2000.4.9

1. Browse the Gallery of Office Assistants and choose one you like.

   a) Set up the Office Assistant's options for the level of help you need.

   b) Hide the Office Assistant.

   c) Retrieve the Office Assistant.

2. Use the Office Assistant to search for Help on using Cut and Paste. Close the Help window when you're through.

Using the Office Proofing Tools

Objective W2000.1.3

No matter how many spelling tests you may have failed in elementary school, you can still produce documents that are free of spelling errors. Word's Spelling feature will flag words as you type by placing a wavy red line underneath possible misspellings: that is, words not in the Office 2000 dictionary.

mispelled

Right-click a flagged word to open the shortcut menu, which lists suggestions for the proper spelling. From the shortcut menu, you can choose the correct spelling, choose to Ignore the word, or Add the spelling to your custom dictionary—a good idea with proper names or unusual words you use frequently.

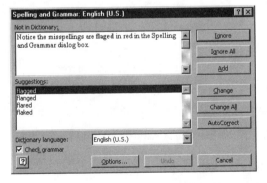

You can check spelling for an entire document by clicking the Spelling button on the Standard toolbar or choosing Tools ➤ Spelling and Grammar. Word reviews your document, and opens the Spelling and Grammar dialog box when it locates words that are not included in the dictionary.

The Spelling and Grammar dialog box gives you all the same options as the Spelling shortcut menu, with a few additions. Here you can choose to ignore all occurrences of the word or choose to change all occurrences to a selected suggested word. You can also manually correct the misspelling and click Change or Change All to move to the next error.

Checking Your Grammar

Objective W2000.1.5

Word's Grammar feature evaluates sentence structure and word usage to determine if you may be making grammatical errors. Word 2000 identifies possible errors on the fly and suggests how you could rewrite the text to make it grammatically correct. In Figure 2.2, Grammar identifies a sentence written in passive voice and makes a suggestion about how the sentence could be reworded to give it more punch.

F I G U R E 2.2: Grammar Checker

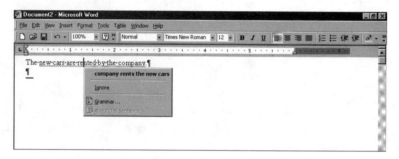

To use Grammar Checker, right-click any word or phrase that has a wavy green line under it. Grammar Checker gives you four options:

- Make one or more suggested corrections
- Leave the text alone
- Open the Grammar dialog box
- Get some additional information about this grammar issue

 Click the About This Sentence button to receive some reference information about this particular grammar problem.

If you would prefer to wait until you have finished entering and editing text to check the spelling and grammar, you can turn off the Automatic Spelling and Grammar option. Choose Tools ➢ Options ➢ Spelling and Grammar and clear the Check Spelling As You Type and the Check Grammar As You Type check boxes.

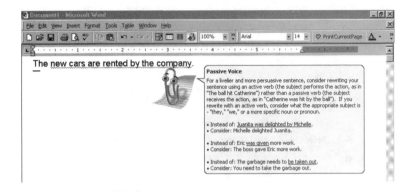

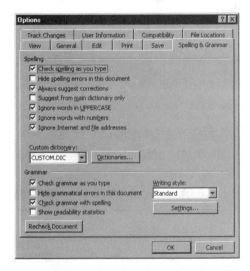

Checking Spelling and Grammar on the Fly

1. Right-click any words that have a wavy line underneath them and choose the correct word or grammar correction from the list.

2. Add words to the Spelling dictionary by clicking the Add button.

3. To see why text was flagged for a grammatical error, click the About This Sentence button.

When you are ready to check your document, click the Spelling and Grammar button on the Standard toolbar. Word will review the entire document and stop at any misspelled words or grammar questions. You can choose to accept or ignore the suggestions. Click Next Sentence to resume the process. If you would prefer not to check the grammar, clear the Check Grammar check box.

WARNING Although Word's Grammar Checker is a dramatic step forward in electronic proofreading, it regularly makes recommendations to fix text that is already correct or misses sentences that are obviously wrong. If you are uncertain, check another grammar reference.

Checking Spelling and Grammar Using the Toolbar

1. Click the Spelling and Grammar button on the Standard toolbar.

2. Accept or ignore any suggested corrections.

3. Click Next Sentence to resume checking.

4. Click Add to add the word to the dictionary.

5. Click Change All or Ignore All to change or ignore all occurrences in the current document.

6. Click the Check Grammar check box to turn off grammar checking.

Spelling and Grammar recognizes more than 80 languages in addition to English. If you type a paragraph in English and then another in Spanish within the same document, Word 2000 will automatically detect the language and use the appropriate spelling and grammar dictionaries.

NOTE To check spelling and grammar in a language other than English, first install the languages you want to use from the Office 2000 Language Pack and install the correct keyboard layout in the Windows Control Panel. In Word Help, search for "Multilanguage" for information on system requirements for each language.

Using the Thesaurus

Objective W2000.1.4

The Thesaurus offers assistance only when called upon. It's there to help you find more descriptive, entertaining, or precise words.

Using the Thesaurus

1. Click the word you want to look up and choose Tools ➢ Language ➢ Thesaurus to open the Thesaurus dialog box, shown in Figure 2.3.

2. Click words in the Meanings column that best represent your context to see synonyms for them. Double-click to get a list of words that have the same or similar meaning.

3. Enter a new word to look up in the Replace with Synonym text box.

4. To review previously looked up words, select from the drop-down list under Looked Up.

F I G U R E 2.3: Thesaurus dialog box

TIP   To quickly find a synonym, right-click a word in your document and choose Synonyms from the shortcut menu.

Hands On

Objectives W2000.1.3. 1.4, and 1.5

1. Start a new document, enter the following text, and then use the Thesaurus (and a bit of humor if you wish) to improve it:

   ```
   Wanted: Fun companion for good times. Any age over
   18 is fine. Must be interesting. Should be cute. Big
   or small, give me a call at 800-555-0000 or send a
   good picture to Nice Person, 555 Pining Away Lane,
   Seattle, WA.
   ```

2. Open a document that contains misspellings. If you don't have any Word 2000 documents with errors (or if you want to pretend that you don't), you can enter the text below in a new document.

   ```
   Every year, several employes are given a specail
   bonus at holiday time. Employees who have done
   exceptoinal jobs are given cars to drive for the
   next year. The new cars are rented by the company.
   The current years cars have to be returned and are
   sold to other employees at a discounted rate. The
   holiday program coresponds to the annual awards
   banquet where many employees are given awards for
   there performance.
   ```

3. Run a spelling and grammar check on the text above (or the document you opened.)

4. Close all open documents, saving changes if you wish.

Using AutoCorrect

Objective W2000.1.16

Office 2000 applications share a feature called AutoCorrect. With Auto-Correct you can build your own list of common misspellings and use that list in Word, Excel, and PowerPoint. Some words, such as *adn* and *teh*, are already in the list. When you accidentally type *adn*, Word automatically changes it to *and*. As you correct misspelled words, you can add them to the AutoCorrect list. AutoCorrect is one of the options in both the Spelling shortcut menu and the Spelling and Grammar dialog box. You can choose Tools ➤ AutoCorrect from the menu to open the dialog box:

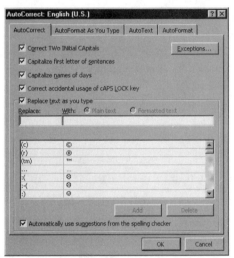

To Create a New AutoCorrect Entry

1. Open the AutoCorrect dialog box by clicking Tools ➤ AutoCorrect.

2. Click in the Replace field and type the entry you want to be automatically corrected.

3. Click in the With field and type the text you want to correct it with.

4. Choose whether you want plain or formatted replacement text.

5. Click Add.

Once you add a word to the AutoCorrect list, you never have to worry about correcting the spelling error again. Also, AutoCorrect recognizes and replaces common combinations of symbols like the copyright symbol (©) and the smilicon now popular online: :-)

A couple of words of caution, though:

- Be sure to verify the correct spelling for words you add to the Auto-Correct list.

- Don't add words that mean something else when you spell them differently. For example, if you commonly reverse the *r* and the *o* in *from*, don't add this error to the AutoCorrect list, or every time you want to type *form* AutoCorrect will automatically change the word to *from*.

There are other AutoCorrect options that you can leave on or turn off based on your personal preference, such as correcting two initial capitals and capitalizing the names of days. (Choose Tools ➤ AutoCorrect to open the AutoCorrect dialog box.) If you want to turn AutoCorrect off entirely, disable the Replace Text As You Type check box. Click the Exceptions button to add:

- abbreviations that you type regularly, so that AutoCorrect doesn't automatically capitalize the next word

- words that require two initial caps, so it doesn't automatically change them

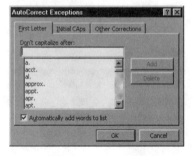

Although AutoCorrect is designed to prevent typing and spelling errors, it is also valuable as a shortcut tool. You can enter words that you type regularly into your AutoCorrect list to save yourself time and keystrokes—long company names, for example, or legal or medical terminology. Just enter a code that you will recognize, such as USA, and AutoCorrect will expand it for you into United States of America. However, if you think you will ever want to use the abbreviation without expanding it, enter a slash (/) or some other character in front of the abbreviation (/USA). Then you can choose whether to have AutoCorrect supply the long form (by typing /USA) or use the abbreviation (by typing USA without the slash).

Hands On

Objectives W2000.1.1 and 1.16

1. Open a new blank document and type a three-sentence paragraph of sample text. Include several proper nouns like your boss's name and company address. Intentionally make at least three spelling errors.

   a) Run the spelling checker and fix your spelling mistakes. Add the proper nouns to the custom dictionary.

   b) Create an AutoCorrect entry for your company's name.

2. Click in the middle of the paragraph you just typed and press the Insert key to change to Overtype mode. (You learned this in Chapter 1.)

   a) Type a short sentence. Note how characters disappear as you type. Press Insert again to return to Insert mode.

   b) Click Undo enough times to replace the text you just overtyped, then click Undo an extra time. Click Redo to cancel out the extra Undo.

3. Click at the bottom of the paragraph and type another sentence. Use the Repeat command to insert the same text into your document twice more. Close without saving.

Adding Pizzazz with Fonts and Formats

One of the primary benefits of using Word 2000 is the ease with which you can give your documents a professional appearance. The right combination of fonts, font styles, sizes, and attributes will make your words jump right off the page.

Fonts and Font Styles

Objectives W2000.1.2 and 1.11

Selecting the right font can be the difference between a professional-looking document and an amateur effort that's tedious to read. Fonts are managed by Windows, which means that a font available in one application is available in all Windows applications. You can access fonts and many of their font attributes from the Formatting toolbar. Word's Formatting toolbar is shown in its entirety in Figure 2.4. If it's sharing a row with the Standard toolbar, you can drag either toolbar elsewhere in the Word window to fully display both toolbars.

F I G U R E 2.4: Word's Formatting toolbar

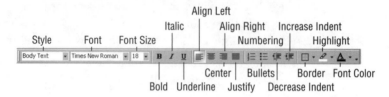

Times New Roman is Word's default font. To change the font, select the text and click the drop-down arrow in the Font control. To change font size, either enter the desired size in the Font Size text box or select one of the sizes in the drop-down list. To turn on Bold, Italics, or Underline, click the corresponding button on the toolbar. Remember that you must select existing text before you can change the font or font style.

To view all of the available font options, choose Format ➤ Font to open the Font dialog box.

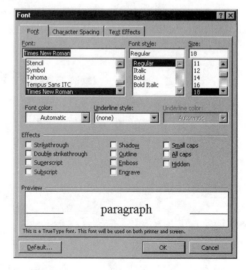

The Font dialog box has three page tabs: Font, Character Spacing, and Text Effects. The Preview window on the Font page lets you see what a font looks like as you apply other options like Font Size, Style, Color, and effects.

Special Text Effects

Objective W2000.1.13

There are 11 effects that you can apply from the Font tab in the Font dialog box. You can use Strikethrough and Double Strikethrough to show proposed deletions in a contract or bylaws. Use Superscript and Subscript to place special characters in formulas (H_2O) and footnotes (as in Miller[1]). Shadow, Outline, Emboss, and Engrave stylize the text so that it stands out, as shown in Figure 2.5.

F I G U R E 2.5: Text effects in Word

Small Caps and All Caps are typically used in stylized documents such as letterheads or business cards. The Small Caps effect converts lowercase letters to smaller versions of the capital letters. To use Small Caps, enter all the text in lowercase and then apply the Small Caps effect.

Hidden text doesn't print and can only be seen when Show/Hide is enabled. This effect was much more commonly applied when there weren't other, more effective ways such as Comments (see Chapter 4) to include nonprinting, invisible document notes.

TIP   Rather than manually marking revised text with Strikethrough, you can use Word 2000's powerful Track Changes feature. Word also has an automatic footnoting system. Both features are discussed in **Chapter 4.**

With the preponderance of inexpensive color printers, being able to add colors to text is an important feature. Font Color is available from the Formatting toolbar as well as in the Font dialog box. There are also many fancy, decorative fonts available in Office 2000, a few of which are shown here.

This is Blackadder JTC.

THIS IS CASTELLAR.

This is Jokerman.

This is Lucida Calligraphy.

This is Ravie.

Character Spacing

Objective W2000.2.3

Use character spacing to adjust the distance between characters. For example, you can spread a title such as *Memorandum* across a page without having to space two or three times between characters.

M E M O R A N D U M

Character spacing is commonly used in advanced desktop publishing when you want to size and scale characters precisely. Select the text you wish to adjust and click Format ➢ Font ➢ Character Spacing. Use the Scaling control if you want specify a percentage for the amount of horizontal space your text currently covers. Word will increase or decrease the between-letter spacing accordingly. Use the Spacing control if you'd like to specify the point distance between letters in your selected text. Adjust Position to move selected text up or down a certain amount of space.

Kerning is also a feature of desktop publishing used with TrueType fonts. Kerning adjusts spacing between certain letter combinations so that letters appear to be more evenly spaced. Enable Kerning by clicking the check box in front of that option then selecting a minimum point size for Word to kern.

Text Effects

On the Text Effects tab you'll find six options designed for documents that will be read on-screen. They cause your text to blink, sparkle, or shimmer: Blinking Background, Las Vegas Lights, Marching Black Ants, Marching Red Ants, Shimmer, and Sparkle Text. To apply one of these special effects, select the text you want to animate, choose Format ➣ Font ➣ Text Effects, and select one of the six options. To turn the special effect off, select the text again and select None from the list of options. A word of advice: if you're going to apply animation, use it sparingly and don't apply it until you are done editing document text. Overdone, it is annoying, and animated documents use more computer resources, slowing down your system.

Highlighting Text for a Distinct Look

Objective W2000.1.7

 If you are creating a document and want to call someone's attention to a particular part of your text, you can *highlight* it so that it stands out for review. This is the computer equivalent of using a highlighter pen on the printout: if you have a color printer, the text will appear highlighted when printed. (Don't overlook the value of highlighting sections of text as a self-reminder.) Select the text you want to highlight and click the drop-down arrow next to the Highlight button to choose and apply a highlight color. The button will save the last chosen pen color, so if you want to use the same color again, just click directly on the Highlight button.

To turn highlighting off, select the highlighted text and choose None from the Highlight button drop-down list. If you prefer, you can choose a color to apply and highlight several sections of text. With no text selected, choose a highlight color. Your mouse pointer changes to an I-beam with highlighter pen attached.

Drag the pen over the text you want to highlight. The highlight pointer will remain active until you click the Highlight button again to turn it off.

Applying Text Enhancements

1. Select the text you want to enhance.

2. Change font, font size, bold, italics, underline, and text color from the Formatting toolbar.

3. Choose Format ➤ Font to open the Font dialog box for more advanced features.

4. Click any of the Effects to turn them on, or clear the check box to turn them off.

5. Click the Character Spacing tab to adjust the settings to expand or condense the characters.

6. Click the Text Effects tab to select from the list of animation options.

7. To highlight text, click the Highlight button and drag it over the text you want to highlight.

Copying Existing Formats

Objective W2000.1.10

Once you have formatted text, there is no need to re-create the format for other text that you want formatted the same way. You can easily copy a format to other text in your document using the Format Painter.

 Select the text with the format you want to copy and click the Format Painter button on the Standard toolbar. Your mouse pointer changes shape to an I-beam with a paintbrush next to it.

Drag the Format Painter I-beam over other text to reformat it to look just like the text you copied. Once you've applied the format, the Format Painter will turn off automatically. If you need to copy the formatting more than once, select the text you want to copy and double-click (instead of single-clicking) the Format Painter button. When you are finished, click the Format Painter button again to turn it off.

The Format Painter not only copies fonts and font attributes but other formatting that you'll learn about in other chapters like line spacing, bullets and numbering, borders and shading, and indents.

Hands On

> **Objectives W2000.1.2, 1.7, 1.10, 1.11, 1.13, and 2.3**

1. Start a new blank document and type a list of your five favorite holidays.

    a) Select the first holiday and make it **bold**.

    b) Select the second holiday and make it 20 point.

    c) Select the third holiday. _Italicize and underline_ it.

    d) Select the fourth holiday and use the Font dialog box to make it 14 point Arial blue.

    e) Use the Format Painter to copy the formatting on the fourth holiday to all the others. Close this document without saving.

2. Enter several lines of text. Highlight a sentence yellow; highlight another lime green. Remove the hightlight.

3. Select another sentence and apply Marching Red Ants to it. Remove the effect.

4. Select a word and make it embossed.

5. Type the following and format for superscripts, subscripts, and other text effects as shown:

    H_2O

    xy^3

    H_2SO_4

    THIS IS AN EXAMPLE OF SMALL CAPS.

    The last word of this sentence is formatted for double ~~strikethrough~~.

6. Select the small caps example from Exercise 5 above. Adjust character spacing to Expanded by 1.2 pts.

Adding Numbers, Symbols, and the Date and Time

When you know how to use some of Word's special formatting features, you can easily create bulleted and numbered lists that have a professional look. Using the Symbol dialog box, you can insert everything from a happy face to the sign for infinity, and you can use Word's date and time features to add the date to a document even if, at the moment, you don't know what month it is.

Numbering and Bullets

Objective W2000.2.2

We live in a world of list makers (even if you ignore late-night talk show hosts), and Word 2000 makes it easy to create bulleted and numbered lists. If you begin a list with a number, Word will number following paragraphs when you press Enter. Begin with an asterisk, and Word will bullet each paragraph.

 To apply numbers to existing text, select the paragraphs and click the Numbering button on the Formatting toolbar. Use the Bullets button to bullet existing paragraphs of text.

Creating a Numbered or Bulleted List

1. If the text you want to number is already entered, highlight the paragraphs to be numbered, and click the Numbering or Bullets button to number or bullet each paragraph.

   OR

1. To automatically number text as you type, type the number 1 and a period, space once, then enter your text for item 1. For bullets, begin with an asterisk and a space.

2. Press Enter. Word will automatically number the next item 2 and press the Numbering button on the Formatting toolbar, or bullet the next item and press the Bullets button.

Creating a Numbered or Bulleted List *(continued)*

3. Continue entering text and pressing the Enter key to create numbered or bulleted points.

4. When you are finished creating the list, press Enter twice to turn automatic numbering or bullets off.

You can also begin numbering by clicking the Numbering button at the beginning of your first paragraph. If you want to use letters rather than numbers in automatic numbering, type A. rather than 1. to begin. Word will number the second and succeeding paragraphs B, C, D, and so on. If you number your first paragraph I, Word will use Roman numerals to number your paragraphs.

Word automatically turns on numbering when you type a paragraph that begins with a number or letter followed by a period, a space, and other text; a period, a tab, and other text; or a tab and other text. You can get out of autonumbering mode by pressing Enter twice after your last numbered item. Since the Numbering button works as a toggle, you can easily convert numbered paragraphs to regular paragraphs by selecting them and clicking the Numbering button.

TIP If automatic numbering or bullets do not work when you follow the steps above, choose Tools ➤ AutoCorrect to open the AutoCorrect dialog box. Make sure that Automatic Bulleted Lists is checked under AutoFormat and Automatic Bulleted Lists and Automatic Numbered Lists are checked under AutoFormat As You Type.

Modifying the Bullet or Number Format

When you use the Bullets and Numbering features, Word supplies a standard, round bullet and leaves a default amount of space between the bullet or number and the text that follows. You can choose a different bullet character, number format, or spacing before entering your list, or you can modify the format of an existing list. If the bulleted or numbered list has already been entered, select the paragraphs you want to change. To change formats, choose Format ➤ Bullets and Numbering to open the Bullets and Numbering dialog box, shown in Figure 2.6.

F I G U R E 2.6: The Bullets and Numbering dialog box

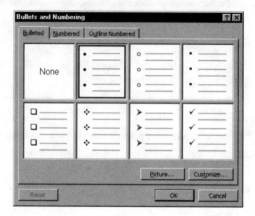

Click the Bulleted, Numbered, or Outline Numbered tab. The dialog box displays seven styles for bulleted text, seven styles for numbered lists, and seven styles for outline numbering. You can simply select any of the styles shown.

TIP See Chapter 3 for information about outlines and outline numbering.

But you aren't limited to the styles shown in the samples. Select the Bulleted tab, and click the Customize button to open the Customize Bulleted List dialog box, as shown in Figure 2.7. (The Customize button will be dimmed if None is selected.)

F I G U R E 2.7: The Customize Bulleted List dialog box

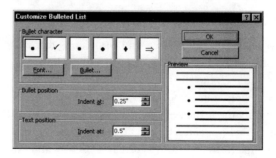

Here you can change the bullet's font by clicking the Font button to open the Font dialog box. You can replace any of the bullet characters that appear here to create your own list of favorites. Click on one of the bullet characters you don't want to use at this time to select it for replacement. Click the Bullet button to open the Symbol dialog box, shown in Figure 2.8.

F I G U R E 2.8: Symbol dialog box

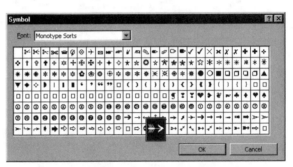

The Font drop-down list contains symbol and display fonts. Choose a font or symbol set from the list, and the characters in the symbol set will be displayed in the *character map* below the drop-down list. Any of the individual characters shown can be used as a bullet character. Click on any character and then click OK to replace the selected bullet character with the symbol you've chosen. You will then be able to select the new symbol from the Bullet Character samples.

TIP If you share documents with others, be sure to select bullets from frequently used fonts or symbol sets (that are installed on their computers), or the bullets will be changed when they open your documents. Symbol, Monotype Sorts, and Wingdings are common symbol sets.

The Bullet Position control lets you change the position of the bullet relative to the left margin. The Text Position control adjusts the position of text relative to the bullet. As you modify the Bullet and Text Position settings, the Preview will change to reflect your modifications.

If you want to use a picture instead of a symbol or character, click the Picture button in the Bullets and Numbering dialog box to open the Insert Picture dialog box, and make a selection.

The Customize Numbered List dialog box, shown in Figure 2.9, works much the same as Customized Bulleted List but there are a few important differences. Here, you can enter a number format such as *Chapter 1*, *Section 1*, or even ____ *1* to create a check-off list. Choose a style from the Number Style drop-down list. You can also have the numbering start at a number other than 1. To change the alignment of the number in the area before the text, click the Number Position drop-down list and choose between Left, Center, and Right.

F I G U R E 2.9: Customize Numbered List dialog box

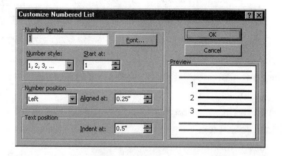

Customizing Number and Bullet Formats

1. Select the list whose numbering or bullet style you want to change.

2. Choose Format ➤ Bullets and Numbering.

3. Make sure the tab you want (Numbered or Bulleted) is displayed.

4. Click a number, letter, or bullet format. To choose a different format, click Customize.

5. Enter a number format, or choose to change the bullet character by clicking the Bullet button. If numbering, enter the starting number if it is other than 1.

Customizing Number and Bullet Formats *(continued)*

6. Adjust the Bullet or Number Position and the Text Position as desired.

7. Click OK to save your changes and return to your document.

To remove numbers and bullets from text, select the bulleted or numbered list and then click the Bullets or Numbering button on the toolbar to turn bullets or numbering off.

Creating Special Characters

Objective W2000.1.15

Many symbols used regularly in business documents aren't on the standard keyboard. Word 2000 makes many of these common symbols available to you with simple keystrokes, and others are available by choosing Insert ➤ Symbol.

Choose Insert ➤ Symbol and select the Symbols tab to open the symbol character map, shown earlier in Figure 2.8. Select the Special Characters tab, shown here:

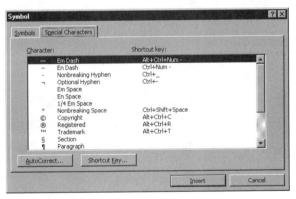

Choose from the symbol font sets or special characters shown and then click the Insert button to insert the symbol into your document. If you need the symbol more than once, copy and paste it to the other locations.

The AutoCorrect method suggested for abbreviations in Chapter 1 can also be applied to create special characters and symbols such as ©, ⊗, and ➜. To add a symbol to the AutoCorrect list, select the symbol and click the AutoCorrect button or choose Tools ➤ AutoCorrect. Enter a character string that will automatically be replaced with the desired symbol—enter (p) for ¶, for example. Make sure it is a character string you don't use in other situations, or you will find it replaced with the symbol every time you type it.

Using Special Characters

1. Choose Insert ➤ Symbol.

2. Choose a symbol from the symbol font sets shown in the character map on the Symbols page or from the list on the Special Characters page.

3. Add regularly used symbols to the AutoCorrect list by clicking Auto-Correct and entering a text string in the Replace text box.

Inserting the Date and Time

Objective W2000.1.14

Word 2000 has 17 different formats you can choose from when inserting the current date and/or time, so the format you want is probably among them. Choose Insert ➤ Date and Time to open the Date and Time dialog box:

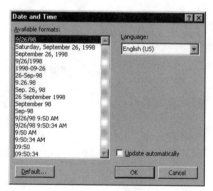

Select a format from the list. If you would like to automatically update the field to the current date and time every time you open the document, click the Update Automatically check box. This inserts the date and time as a field rather than as text. A *field* serves as a placeholder that is replaced with current data. (Be careful not to use this option when the date on a document is important to mark a paper trail.) A Date and Time field is most useful when a document is in draft form and you want to know when it was last worked on, or when a memo or notice is regularly printed and mailed and should always have the current date. The Date and Time field is only updated when you print the document, re-open the document, or right-click on the field and choose Update Field. Go to Print Preview to see the changed date and time. When you return to the document, the date and time will be updated.

Inserting the Date and Time

1. Choose Insert Date and Time.

2. Select the desired Date and Time format.

3. Click the Update Automatically check box if you want to insert the date and time as a field.

4. Click OK to insert the date and time into your document.

Hands On

Objectives W2000.1.14, 1.15, and 2.2

1. Enter a list of at least 10 things you have to do this week.

   a) Select the list and turn on Numbering. Select the list again and turn on Bullets.

   b) Change the bullet characters to some other symbol, such as a right-pointing arrow.

2. Type a new list below the To Do list that includes things you need to buy or errands you need to run. Start by entering the number 1, a period, and a space. When you press Enter after the first item, the number 2 should appear and a tab should be automatically inserted after each of the two numbers. If Automatic Numbering is not turned

on, go to Format ➤ AutoFormat to open the AutoFormat dialog box. Click Options to open the AutoCorrect dialog box, click the AutoFormat As You Type tab, and make sure Automatic Bulleted Lists and Automatic Numbered Lists are checked.

3. On a new blank line, choose Insert ➤ Symbol and insert a symbol or special character that you might use often. Add it to the AutoCorrect list so you can type a few characters and have them replaced with the symbol. After you have entered it, type the characters and see if AutoCorrect changes them to your symbol.

4. In the same document:

   a) Use Ctrl+Home to move to the top of your document. Choose Insert ➤ Date and Time to add the date and time to your document in a format that includes the time. Enable Update Automatically.

   b) Below the Date and Time field, choose Insert ➤ Date and Time again but do not enable Update Automatically. Save and close the document. Wait a couple of minutes and re-open the document. Switch to Print Preview and zoom in on the date and time. The first time will reflect the current time, and the second time should still reflect the time the field was originally entered.

Aligning and Formatting Paragraphs

In addition to formatting text or characters, skilled Word users must know how to format lines and paragraphs of text. In this section, you'll learn how to use indents and tabs and to control how text flows on the page.

Aligning Text

Objective W2000.2.1

Word has four ways (see Figure 2.10) to align text: left, center, right, and full (justify).

To align text, position the insertion point anywhere in the paragraph and click one of the alignment buttons on the Formatting toolbar:

F I G U R E 2.10: Aligning paragraph text

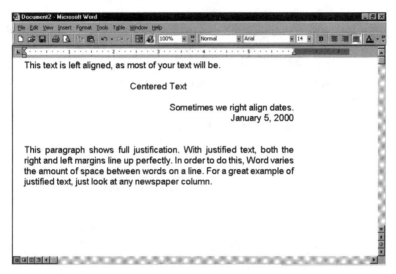

Using Indentation Options

Objective W2000.2.5

Word offers three ways to access the paragraph-indenting features: the Formatting toolbar, the ruler, and the Paragraph dialog box.

You'll find the easiest method to change indents on the Formatting toolbar. Click anywhere in the paragraph you want to indent or select multiple paragraphs, and click the Decrease Indent button to reduce the left indent by 1/2 inch. Click the Increase Indent button to extend the indent by 1/2 inch.

Creating Indents Using the Ruler

The second method of indenting paragraphs—using the ruler—can take a little work to master but is a very visual way to set left, right, hanging, and dual indents. You can use the ruler to set tabs as well as indents and left and right margins in Page Layout view.

TIP If you prefer to do most of your work without the ruler, turn the ruler off by choosing View ➤ Ruler to remove the check. To make the ruler temporarily visible, point to the narrow gray line under the command bars and the ruler will reappear. As soon as the pointer moves back to your document, the ruler will slide back under the command bars.

There are four indent markers on the ruler, shown in Figure 2.11:

- A *first line indent* works the same as pressing Tab on the keyboard.

- A *hanging indent* (sometimes called an outdent) "hangs" the remaining lines in a paragraph to the right of the first line when this marker is positioned to the right of the first line indent marker.

- A *left indent* sets a paragraph off from the rest of the text by moving all lines in from the left margin.

- A *right indent* moves text in from the right margin and is typically combined with a left indent to make a *dual indent*. Dual indents are used most commonly to set off block quotations.

F I G U R E 2.11: Indent markers on the ruler

Hanging Indent   First Line Indent

Left Indent   Right Indent

To change the indents for existing text, select the paragraph or paragraphs you want to indent and drag the indent marker on the ruler to the desired location. Moving the first line or the hanging indent marker indents or outdents the first line of each paragraph. Moving the left or right indent marker indents all lines of each paragraph.

If you forget which marker is which, point to any of them for a moment and view the ScreenTip. You can use the ruler to set indents before entering text. Position the insertion point where you plan to enter the new text.

The indents will apply to all newly entered text until you change the indent settings.

Indenting Using the Toolbar and Ruler

1. Click in the paragraph you want to indent, and click the Increase Indent button or the Decrease Indent button on the Formatting toolbar.

2. To use the ruler: change to Normal view and turn the ruler on if it is not already visible (choose View ➤ Ruler).

3. Select the text you want to indent.

4. Drag the first line indent marker to the right to indent the first line in a paragraph.

5. Drag the hanging indent marker to the right to indent all but the first line in a paragraph.

6. Drag the left indent marker to indent all the selected text.

7. Drag the right indent marker to indent the selected text from the right margin.

If you select paragraphs that do not share the same indent settings, one or all of the indent markers on the ruler will be dimmed. Click the dimmed marker(s) to make the indent settings the same for all the selected paragraphs.

Indenting Using the Paragraph Dialog Box

The third way to set indents is by using the Paragraph dialog box, shown in Figure 2.12. To access the dialog box, choose Format ➤ Paragraph or right-click and choose Paragraph from the shortcut menu.

On the Indents and Spacing tab, click the up and down arrows next to the Left and Right text boxes (called *spin boxes* because you can "spin" through the options), or enter decimal numbers directly in the text boxes. In the Special control, you can select First Line or Hanging to indent or outdent the first line of the paragraphs by 1/2 inch. If you want the indent to be more or less than 0.5 inch, enter the special indent value in the By control.

FIGURE 2.12: The Paragraph dialog box

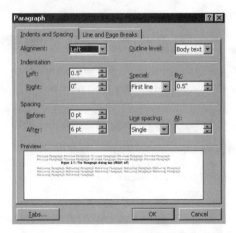

Indenting Using the Paragraph Dialog Box

1. Select the text you want to indent and open the Paragraph dialog box (choose Format ➢ Paragraph or right-click and choose **Paragraph**).

2. Use the spin box controls to change the Left and Right indent settings.

3. Click the Special drop-down arrow to select First Line or Hanging indent.

4. Click OK to close the Paragraph dialog box and see your changes.

Setting Line Spacing Options

Objective W2000.2.3

Word 2000 provides six options for adjusting *line spacing*, the vertical distance between lines of text:

> **Single:** Enough room to comfortably display the largest character on a line

> **1.5 lines:** one-and-a-half single lines

Double: Twice as much room as single spacing

At Least: A minimum line spacing for the selection

Exactly: Makes all lines evenly spaced regardless of the size of the fonts or graphics included in those lines

Multiple: Used to enter line spacing other than single, 1.5, and double

To change the line spacing for existing text, select the paragraphs you want to change. Open the Paragraph dialog box (choose Format ➤ Paragraph or right-click and select Paragraph from the shortcut menu), and click the drop-down list to select from the line-spacing options:

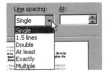

At Least and Exactly require you to enter a point size in the At text box. Multiple requires you to enter the amount by which to multiply. For example, you can triple-space selected paragraphs by choosing Multiple and then entering 3 in the At control.

Setting Line Spacing

1. Select the text whose line spacing you want to change.

2. Choose Format ➤ Paragraph to open the Paragraph dialog box. Click the Indents and Spacing tab if the page is not visible.

3. Click the Line Spacing drop-down list to select the desired line spacing.

4. If you are choosing At Least, Exactly, or Multiple, enter a number in the At control.

5. Click OK to return to the document and review the changes.

To see all the formatting that is applied to a paragraph, choose Help ➤ What's This? and click on the paragraph. You'll get an information box, such as the one shown below, that displays paragraph and font formatting related to the paragraph. Choose Help ➤ What's This? again to turn it off.

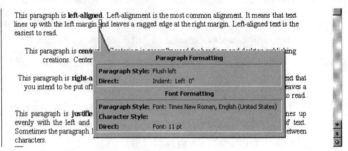

Using Tabs

▶ *Objective W2000.2.6*

Tab stops are markers set by default at half-inch intervals across the width of the document. Pressing the Tab key moves the cursor from one tab stop to the next. One of the most common uses of a tab is to indent the first line of a paragraph.

Tabs are also used to create *parallel columns*, vertically aligning text within a document. You can change the tab-stop settings by using the ruler or the Tabs dialog box. Setting the stops includes choosing the alignment type and location for each tab stop you want to use. Figure 2.13 shows the five basic types of tab stops:

Left: The default type. Text appears to the right of the tab stop.

Center: Text is automatically adjusted to the left and the right of the tab stop until it is centered under the tab stop.

Right: Text appears to the left of the tab stop.

Decimal: Used for numeric entries. Text lines up with the decimal point.

Bar: Inserts a vertical line in your document at the tab stop. In earlier versions of Word, the Bar tab was used to create a vertical separator for columns. With Word 2000, you can do this automatically when you set up columns.

F I G U R E   2.13: Four of the five types of tab stops were used to align these

TUESDAY'S SCHEDULE			
Employee	**Shift Responsibility**	**Shift Hours**	**Rate**
Jeff Morse	stock shelves	7:30 a.m. – 2:30 p.m.	$7.50
Jessica Beecham	next weeks' schedule	10:00 a.m. – 5:30 p.m.	$8.25
Sean Callan	purchasing	12:00 p.m. – 9:30 p.m.	$10.00
Seneca Sojourn	order shipping	5:00 p.m. – 1:30 a.m.	$8.50

Setting Tab Stops Using the Ruler

At the left end of the ruler in Print Layout view is a Tab Selection button that allows you to select the type of tab you want to set. By default it is set on Left Tab. Click the button to toggle through the five tab choices:

Once you have chosen the type of tab you want to set, click on the ruler to set a tab. The tab-stop marker appears, and all the tabs to the left of the marker are deleted. If you want to move the tab stop, click on the marker and drag it to a new location on the ruler.

If you want the tab stops to apply to existing text, be sure to select the text first—before clicking the ruler. Unless you select the entire document or the last paragraph in the document, the tab stops will only apply to the selected paragraph(s). You can, however, set the tab stops for a blank document before you start entering text, and then the tab stops can be used throughout the document. To clear a tab stop, point to the tab stop and simply drag it off the ruler.

Setting Tabs Using the Ruler

1. Click the Tab Selection button at the left end of the ruler to toggle through the five tab choices.

2. Click the ruler to set the tab stops—all the default tab stops to the left of the new tabs are deleted.

3. Drag the tab-stop marker on the ruler to change the tab position.

4. Drag the tab-stop marker off the ruler to remove the tab stop.

TIP   If you're using tabs to create parallel columns, you may not be using the most efficient tool. In most situations, it is easier to create parallel columns using Word's Tables feature. See Chapter 3 for information regarding tables.

Setting Tab Stops and Leaders Using the Tabs Dialog Box

Objective W2000.2.8

You can also create tab stops using the Tabs dialog box. Make sure the insertion point is located where you want the new tab stops to begin. (If the text you want to format is already entered, select it.) Access the Tabs dialog box, shown in Figure 2.14, by choosing Format ➤ Tabs.

F I G U R E 2.14: The Tabs dialog box

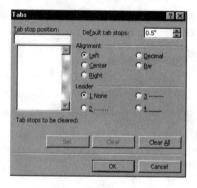

In the Tab Stop Position text box, type the location for the tab stop you want to create. In the Alignment control, choose how you want text to align at the tab stop. The Leader control lets you select a *leader* to lead the reader's eye across the text. The leader (see Figure 2.15) precedes the tabbed text.

When you have set the position, type, and leader (if you wish) for the tab stop, click the Set button. The new tab stop will be added to the tab-stop list. Repeat these steps to set any other tab stops.

F I G U R E 2.15: Tab stops and leaders

Vacation Schedule by Month

Frank.. May
Rebecca.. June
Sherry.. June
Janis .... July
James .... August
Richard.. August

You can also use the dialog box to change an existing tab stop. Select the tab stop from the list below the Tab Stop Position control. Change the Alignment and Leader options; then click Set. To remove an existing tab stop, select it from the list and click the Clear button. Clicking Clear All removes all the tab stops you added, reverting to the default tab settings. When you are done setting tab stops, click OK to close the Tabs dialog box.

Setting Tabs and Leaders Using the Tabs Dialog Box

1. Open the Tabs dialog box by choosing Format ➢ Tabs.

2. Type a decimal value in the Tab Stop Position text box.

3. Select an alignment style and, optionally, a leader style.

4. Click OK.

5. Enter text, pressing Tab between each column.

To see where tabs have been typed in existing text, click the Show/Hide Paragraph Marks button on the Standard toolbar. You'll see a right-pointing arrow to indicate a tab:

TUESDAY'S·SCHEDULE¶

•Employee		Shift·Responsibility		Shift·Hours		Rate¶
Jeff·Morse	→	stock·shelves	→	7:30·a.m.–2:30·p.m.	→	$7.50¶
Jessica·Beecham	→	next·weeks'·schedule	→	10:00·a.m.–5:30·p.m.	→	$8.25¶
Sean·Callan	→	purchasing	→	12:00·p.m.–9:30·p.m.	→	$10.00¶
Seneca·Sojourn	→	order·shipping	→	5:00·p.m.–1:30·a.m.	→	$8.50¶

Hands On

▶ ***Objectives W2000.2.1, 2.3, 2.5, and 2.6***

1. In a new document, set tabs to enter the text below in parallel columns. Set a right tab for the times and center the number of weeks. Save the document as Class Schedule.

Class	Day	Time	Weeks
Access	Monday	1 p.m.–3 p.m.	10
Excel	Tuesday	11 a.m.–2 p.m.	7
FrontPage	Friday	8 a.m.–4 p.m.	2
PowerPoint	Monday	5 p.m.–7 p.m.	4
Outlook	Saturday	9 a.m.–5 p.m.	1
Word	Thursday	7 a.m.–10 a.m.	7

2. In a new document, enter the following text and format each paragraph as described in the paragraph.

A first line indent works the same as pressing the Tab key on the keyboard. Single-line spacing provides enough room to comfortably display the largest character on a line.

A hanging indent (sometimes called an outdent) "hangs" the first line of a paragraph to the left of the remaining lines. Double spacing provides twice as much room between lines of text as single spacing.

A left indent sets a paragraph off from the rest of the text by moving all lines in from the left margin. Line spacing of 1.5 leaves one-and-a-half single lines between each line of text.

A right indent moves text in from the right margin and is typically combined with a left indent to make a dual indent. Dual indents, like the dual indent used in this

paragraph, are used most commonly to set off block quotations. Multiple line spacing is used to specify the
number of lines: in this paragraph, 3 lines.

3. In a new document, set a left tab at .5, a center tab at 2, a right tab
at 4.25, and decimal tab at 5, and then enter the schedule information shown in the graphic above this Hands On section or similar
text of your own.

Select the line of column headings and change the tab stop for Shift
Hours to a Center tab and the tab stop for Rate to a Right tab. Move
both tabs so that the headings line up appropriately with the columns.

4. Press Ctrl+Home to navigate to the top of your document. Press
Enter twice to leave some space, then insert a heading above the text
you entered in Exercise 3 above. Change the heading to right-aligned,
then change it to centered.

5. Select the text from Exercise 4 above and set line spacing for 1.5.
Experiment with justification using the text you entered in Exercise
2 above. Do you prefer left-aligned or justified?

Replacing and Checking Text

As you create documents in Word, you may want to use the same text in
another document or correct an error that occurs several times. Word
2000 offers several features to help you replace and check text—including
grammar—efficiently. As you know, there's even a Thesaurus to help you
find that perfectly descriptive word or phrase.

Creating and Applying Frequently Used Text

Objective W2000.1.16

Word has two features that let you easily insert frequently used text and
graphics. The first option, AutoCorrect, is included in Chapter 1 because
it is common to all Office 2000 applications. The second feature, *Auto-
Text*, is particular to Word and allows you to store formatted text or
graphics, even entire paragraphs, and then recall them with a couple of
keystrokes.

To create an AutoText entry, select the text you want to store as Auto-Text. To include the text's format such as font and font style, before selecting, click the Show/Hide Paragraph Marks button on the Standard toolbar and make sure you include the paragraph mark in the selection. Choose Insert ➤ AutoText ➤ New to create the entry (see Figure 2.16). You will be prompted to give the entry a name—make it short and easy to remember, but at least 4 characters long. To insert the AutoText in a document, type the name you assigned to the entry and press the F3 key.

F I G U R E 2.16: Creating AutoText

Word provides a number of canned AutoText entries that you can access from the Insert ➤ AutoText menu:

Just choose a category, and then select the entry you want to insert into your document.

TIP If you're inserting a lot of AutoText into a document, you can turn on the AutoText toolbar by choosing View Toolbars ➤ AutoText. The toolbar's All Entries drop-down menu is the same as the menu bar's AutoText menu.

Delete AutoText entries on the AutoText tab of the AutoCorrect dialog box (choose Insert ➤ AutoText ➤ AutoText) by selecting the entry you want to delete and clicking the Delete button:

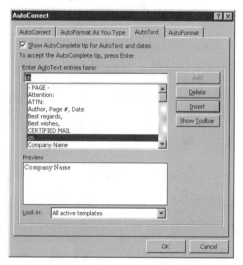

Creating, Inserting, and Deleting AutoText

1. Select the text to include in the AutoText. To include formatting, click the Show/Hide Paragraph Marks button and select the text, including the paragraph mark.

2. Choose Insert ➤ AutoText ➤ New and name the AutoText.

3. To insert the AutoText in a document, type the entry's name and press the F3 key.

4. To delete an AutoText entry, click the AutoText button on the toolbar to open the AutoCorrect dialog box to the AutoText tab. Select an AutoText entry and click the Delete button.

Finding and Replacing Text

Objective W2000.1.12

When you are working with a long document, one of the fastest ways to make repetitive changes to a document is through Find and Replace. Find helps you locate a *text string*, and Replace substitutes new text for the existing string.

Using Find

 To locate a word or phrase, click the Select Browse Object button and choose Find. Click the More button to see all the available options in the Find and Replace dialog box, shown in Figure 2.17.

F I G U R E   2.17: Find and Replace dialog box

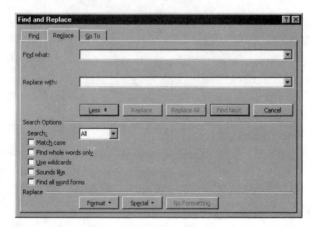

Enter the text you want to locate in the Find What text box. You can have Word search the entire document (All), or for faster searching, just choose to search above (Up) or below (Down) the insertion point. You can also search for words that are in the same case as you entered (Match Case).

Objective W2000E.2.6

To specify a particular format, or to find special characters or non-printing elements such as paragraph marks and spaces, click the Format or the Special button at the bottom of the dialog box. Choose the type of format, such as Font, and then identify the specific format (for example, Times New Roman) you want to search for. If it's a special or non-printing character you want, click the Special button and then choose the character from the list of choices. Using this option, you can, for example, search for every place you entered two hard returns after a paragraph or every section break.

When you have entered your Search options, click the Find Next button to identify the first occurrence of the text string. You can then close the Find dialog box and use the blue Browse buttons at the bottom of the vertical scroll bar to move to previous or next occurrences of the string.

Using Replace

Replace allows you to replace one or all occurrences of a word or phrase with different text. Let's say you just finished a lengthy proposal for a client and you realize you've misspelled their company name throughout. Sure, you could correct each misspelling individually, but why? Click Edit ➢ Replace, and Word opens the Replace tab of the Find and Replace dialog box. Type the incorrectly spelled company name in the Find What field, and the correctly-spelled company name in the Replace With field. Click Replace All, and Word does the work for you.

Use Replace with the Format and Special buttons to replace every place you used Times New Roman 12 pt. font, for example, with Comic Sans 14 pt., or every occurrence of two paragraph marks with one.

Finding and Replacing Text

1. Click the Select Browse Object button and the Find button to open the Find dialog box.

2. Enter the characters you want to search for in the Find What text box. Click Find Next.

3. Close the Find dialog box and click the Next Find/Go To button at the bottom of the vertical scroll bar. Browse through each of the occurrences of the text string.

4. To replace text, open the Find dialog box again and click the Replace tab.

5. Enter the text string you want to search for in the Find What text box and the characters you want to replace it with in the Replace With text box.

6. Click Replace All to complete the replace operation in one step. If you want to review each replacement, choose Replace. Click Find Next to locate the next occurrence. You may need to reposition the dialog box to see the text. Click Replace until you have made all the replacements.

Inserting Page Breaks

Objective W2000.1.6

Word paginates documents automatically—when text exceeds the length of a page, Word moves to the next page by inserting a soft page break. After you've previewed your document, you might decide you want a page to break earlier: at the end of a cover page, or just before a new topic. To insert a *hard page break* that forces the page to break at the insertion point's current location, press Ctrl+Enter.

Changing Page Orientation and Paper Size

Objective W2000.3.6

If you think that your document would look better in *landscape* orientation (11 × 8.5) than *portrait* (8.5 × 11), you can change the orientation in Page Setup. Choose File ➢ Page Setup ➢ Paper Size or double-click on the gray frame at the top of the ruler bar to open the dialog box.

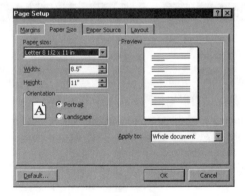

You can also change to another paper size entirely, including a custom size for nonstandard forms such as note cards or half-sheets. If you choose custom size, enter the dimensions for height and width.

Objective W2000.3.16

If you want to apply a page-size change to only part of your document, position the insertion point at the beginning of the page you want to change, go to Page Setup, change the page size, and choose This Point Forward in the Apply To control. To apply the change to a single page and not all the pages that follow it, move the insertion point to the end of the last page with this formatting, select This Point Forward, and change back to the original paper size.

Changing Page Orientation and Paper Size

1. To change page orientation for the entire document, choose File ➢ Page Setup ➢ Paper Size.

2. Click the Portrait or Landscape Orientation option.

3. To change paper size, click the Paper Size drop-down list and select an option. If you choose Custom, enter the dimensions of the paper in the Height and Width text boxes.

4. To change page orientation for only part of a document, choose This Point Forward in the Apply To text box.

Aligning Text Vertically

Objective W2000.3.11

After you have the page orientation and paper size set, you may want to create a title page for your document. One easy way to do this is to enter the text you want on the title page and then center text vertically on the page between the top and bottom margins. To activate this feature, position the insertion point on the page you want to align. Choose File ➢ Page Setup and click the Layout tab. Under Vertical Alignment, you will find four options:

Top: The default setting, text lines up with the top margin.

Center: Text on the page is centered between the top and bottom margins.

Justified: Text is spread out so that each line is the same distance apart with the top line at the top margin and the bottom line at the bottom margin.

Bottom: Text lines up with the bottom margin.

Aligning Text Vertically

1. Click on the page that contains the text you want to align.

2. Choose File ➢ Page Setup ➢ Layout and choose Top, Center, Justified, or Bottom from the Vertical Alignment drop-down list. Click OK.

Setting Margins

Objective W2000.3.7

Word's default *margins*, the white space between text and the edge of the paper the text will be printed on, are 1 inch on the top and bottom and 1.25 inches on the left and right sides of the page. To change margins, use the Margins page of the Page Setup dialog box, shown in Figure 2.18 and set the following options:

Top, Bottom, Left, and Right spin box controls set the amount of white space on the four edges of the document.

The *gutter margin* is used to add additional space to a document that will be bound.

The *mirror margins* feature helps you format margins for back-to-back printing.

The default for the Apply To control is Whole Document. You can, however, change margins from the insertion point forward for the rest of a document by choosing This Point Forward from the Apply To drop-down list.

If you prefer, you can change margins using the vertical and horizontal rulers in Print Preview or in Print Layout view. Point to the margin line on the ruler and the pointer changes to a double-headed arrow. When you hold down the mouse button, a dotted line extends through the document, showing the location of the margin. Drag the dotted line in the desired direction to adjust the margin.

F I G U R E   2.18: Page Setup dialog box, Margins tab

Changing Document Margins

1. Position the insertion point where you want the margin changes to take effect.

2. Choose File ➢ Page Setup to open the Page Setup dialog box, and click the Margins tab.

3. Click the Mirror Margins check box to activate mirror margins, if desired.

4. Use the spin box arrows or type in the text boxes to increase or decrease the margins.

5. Click OK to return to the document.

Getting into Print

Although we are transmitting more and more documents electronically these days, we still print a lot of documents. In this section, we'll look at your printing options and also discuss how to print envelopes and labels, a handy feature for home and office work.

Using Print Preview

Objective W2000.3.2

Previewing your document before printing it gives you the chance to see how the pages break and whether there are any layout problems that will make the document look less than its best.

As you learned in Chapter 1, you can preview any document by clicking the Print Preview button on the Standard toolbar or choosing File ➢ Print Preview.

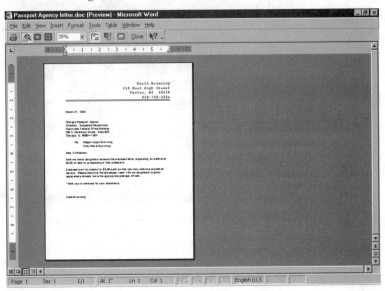

Table 2.1 shows the options available in Print Preview.

T A B L E 2.1: Options in Print Preview

Button	Button Name	Placeholder
	Print	Prints the document.
	Magnify	When pressed, click on the document to zoom in or out. Inactivate to edit the document.
	One Page	Shows only one page of the document.
	Multiple Page	Shows a maximum of six pages at one time.
50%	Zoom	Changes the magnification level.

T A B L E   2.1:   Options in Print Preview   *(continued)*

Button	Button Name	Placeholder
	View Ruler	Turns the vertical and horizontal rulers on and off.
	Shrink to Fit	Reduces the document by one page to prevent spill-over.
	Full Screen	Turns full-screen mode on.
	Close	Closes Print Preview.
	Context-Sensitive Help	Click Help, and then click any button within Print Preview to activate Help about that button.

Printing Options

Objective W2000.3.1

As you learned in Chapter 1, when you click the Print button on the Standard toolbar, Word uses the current print options. By default, one copy of the document is sent to the Windows default printer. If you want to change the print settings, choose File ➢ Print to open the Print dialog box:

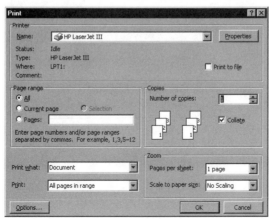

In the Print dialog box you can:

- Choose another printer

- Print only designated pages of a document, including current page, a range of pages, or selected text

- Choose to print the document properties (who created it, when it was created, how many words, characters, and so on) or other lists such as AutoText entries

- Indicate in the Print text box whether to print just even pages, just odd pages, or both

- Specify the number of copies and have them collated (pages 1, 2, 3 for each copy rather than all copies of page 1, then all copies of page 2, etc.)

- Print to a file so that someone without Word 2000 can print the document

Set the print options the way you want them and click Print to send the document to the printer.

NOTE   You can also print 2, 4, 6, 8, or 16 pages to a sheet. In the Zoom section of the Print dialog box, select the number of pages from the Pages per Sheet drop-down list, and select the paper size from the Scale to Paper Size drop-down list.

Creating and Printing Envelopes and Labels

▶ *Objective W2000.3.14*

One of the time-saving features of Office 2000 is its ability to maintain address books that are shared among the applications. (See *Mastering Microsoft Outlook 2000*—also from Sybex—for information about Outlook address books.) Combine that with Word's Envelopes and Labels feature, and it has never been easier to prepare documents for mailing. Even if you're not using an address book, Word makes it a snap to produce envelopes and mailing labels.

Creating and Printing an Envelope

1. If you are writing a letter, enter the name and address you want on the envelope as the inside address in the letter.

2. Choose Tools ➢ Envelopes and Labels and choose the Envelopes tab, shown in Figure 2.19.

3. The name and address you entered should appear in the Delivery Address box. If it does not, close the dialog box, copy the name and address, reopen the dialog box, and use Ctrl+V or Shift+Ins to paste it.

4. Choose to enter or omit a return address.

5. Click the Options button to open the Envelope Options dialog box.

6. Click the Envelopes Options tab to set envelope options such as envelope size, delivery point bar code, and fonts.

7. Click the Printing Options tab to set printing options such as feed method and the printer tray that contains the envelope, and click OK.

8. Click the Print button to send the envelope to the printer.

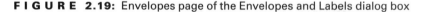

F I G U R E 2.19: Envelopes page of the Envelopes and Labels dialog box

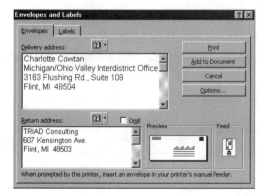

TIP   If you want your return address to appear as the default in the Envelopes and Labels dialog box, choose Tools ➢ Options ➢ User Information and enter your mailing address.

The Labels feature gives you the option to print one label or a full page of the same label. (See Chapter 4 for information about creating individualized labels for different people.) Click the Labels tab of the Envelopes and Labels dialog box (choose Tools ➤ Envelopes and Labels to get you there).

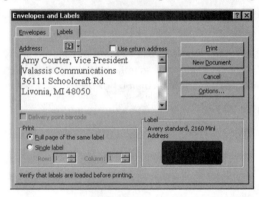

Choose whether you would like a full page of the same label or a single label. You can even specify which row and column to print on so you can use up those partial sheets of labels left over from other printing jobs. If you want to print a full page of return address labels, click the Use Return Address check box.

The default label is Avery standard, 2160 Mini Address. If this is not the kind of label you use, click the Options button to select a different label:

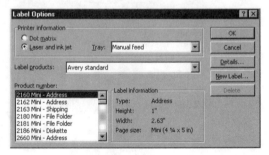

Choose the product and product number you want to use from the list provided. Click the Details button to see the actual measurements and layout of the labels you have selected or the New Label button to design custom labels. Click OK to close either page and OK again to return to the Envelopes and Labels dialog box.

You can now print the labels. If you are creating return address labels or labels that you want to save, click the New Document button to paste the labels into a new document. Save the document before sending the labels to the printer. In the future, to print more of the same labels, you can open the label document and print it without having to recreate the labels.

Creating and Printing Labels

1. Choose Tools ➢ Envelopes and Labels ➢ Labels.

2. Enter any changes to the Address box. Click Use Return Address if you want to create return address labels.

3. Check if you want to print a Full Page of the Same Label or a Single Label.

4. Click the Options button to select a different label product or to change the printer information.

5. Click the Details or New Label button to adjust the dimensions of the labels selected.

6. Close the New Label or Details page and the Labels Options page by clicking OK or Cancel.

7. Click the Print button to send the labels to the printer or the New Document button to create a label document that can be saved for re-use.

Hands On

Objectives W2000.1.6, 1.12, 3.1, 3.2, 3.6, 3.7, 3.11, 3.14, and 3.16

1. Open an existing Word document and change the margins to 1 inch top, bottom, left, and right for the entire document.

   a) Insert a hard page break at the end of the document and type a short sentence on your new page. Apply a portrait orientation to the new page.

b) Insert another hard page break at the beginning of the document. Create a title page for this document with your name and today's date (inserted as a field.)

c) Vertically align the text on the title page only.

d) View your document in Print Preview, two pages at a time. Close the preview.

e) Navigate to page 1 of your document (the title page) and print just that page.

f) Print the rest of the document (without the title page).

g) Close this document without saving your changes.

2. Create and print an envelope that includes your return address.

3. Create a full page of return labels for yourself. Create and save a new document containing the labels.

4. Type a letter and create an envelope for it that you add to your document. Preview it in Print Preview before printing it.

5. Type the following text in a new Word document. (You may have saved this text from an earlier exercise. If so, open it.) Then use Find and Replace to change all occurrances of *car* to *automobile*.

Every year, several employees are given special bonuses at holiday time. Employees who have done exceptional jobs are given cars to drive for the next year. The new cars are rented by the company. The current year's cars have to be returned and are sold to other employees at a discounted rate. The holiday program corresponds to the annual awards banquet, where many employees are given awards for their performance.

CHAPTER

3

**Applying Advanced
Formatting Techniques**

When you're comfortable with the basics, you'll soon find yourself looking for ways to enhance the appearance of text. Word features such as tables, columns, outlines, and templates become important as you move beyond simply typing text that wraps at the margin. In this chapter, you will learn to format pages and set text flow options. You'll be impressed with the styles, templates, and shortcuts available in Word, and you'll learn to use Word's advanced formatting tools to create eye-catching documents.

Formatting Pages

Page numbers, headers, and footers make a lengthy document easier to follow. Word 2000 can help you with everything from automatically numbering the pages to inserting different headers and footers on odd and even pages. You can also adjust hyphenation and other text flow options to make sure your final document looks its best.

Formatting Sections

Objective W2000.3.16

Word 2000 organizes the formatting for documents in sections. A *section* is a part of a document that has a specified number of columns and that uses a common set of margins, page orientation, headers and footers, and sequence of page numbers. Word automatically inserts section breaks when you:

- Format text as columns (see "Working with Columns" later in this chapter)

- Change Page Setup options and indicate that you want the changes to apply from This Point Forward

---

TIP   You will want to manually insert a section break to apply different page size or header and footer formatting within a document.

Section breaks can be seen in Normal view by default and in other views by clicking the Show/Hide button on the Standard toolbar to view non-printing characters. Breaks appear as double-dotted lines with the words "Section Break" and the type of break in them:

Inserting and Deleting Section Breaks

1. Move the insertion point to where you'd like the break and choose Insert ➤ Break.

2. Choose where you'd like the next section to begin by selecting one of the four section options in the Break dialog box.

3. Switch to Normal view to see the section breaks in your document, or click the Show/Hide button on the Standard toolbar.

4. To delete a section break, select it and press the Delete key.

Creating and Modifying Page Numbers

Objectives W2000.3.5 and 3.9

Whether or not you have inserted section breaks, you may want a simple way to automatically number the pages. Nothing could be more effortless than Word's Page Numbering feature. Choose Insert ➤ Page Numbers to open the Page Numbers dialog box, shown in Figure 3.1.

F I G U R E 3.1: Page Numbers dialog box

You have four options:

Position—Bottom of Page or Top of Page

Alignment—Left, Center, Right, Inside, or Outside (use Inside or Outside when you have enabled mirror margins in Page Setup)

Show Number on First Page—Toggle on or off

Format—Opens the Page Number Format dialog box:

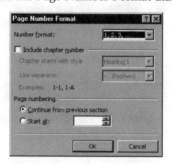

The Page Number Format dialog box allows you to choose a numbering style such as "A, B, C" or "1, 2, 3," and to include a chapter number, if you desire. You could, for example, click the Include Chapter Number check box to show 1–1 as the chapter and page number. If you would like to start your page numbering at a number other than 1, enter a number in the Start At text box. Once you have made your formatting choices, click OK to return to the Page Numbers dialog box and OK again to insert the page numbers. To view the page numbers, switch to Print Layout view or Print Preview.

Setting Up Different Page Numbering

Objective W2000E.2.2

If your document has more than one section, you can set up different page numbering for each section. Position the insertion point on the first page of the document (which is the beginning of the first section) and add page numbering. Then move the insertion point to the first page of the *second* section, and choose Insert ➣ Page Numbers again. Click Format to set up the formatting for this section's numbering. If you want the page numbering to continue from the first section, choose that option in the Page Number Format dialog box. Repeat the process for any additional sections. If you want to remove page numbers, you need to edit the header or footer where the page number appears (see the next section).

Creating Headers and Footers

Objective W2000.3.10

Page numbers are certainly useful, but you'll probably also want to include other information on each page—All Rights Reserved, your name, or the name of your company, for example. For this type of information, use the Header and Footer feature. Headers and footers are placed in the top and bottom margins. To insert a header or footer, choose View ➤ Header and Footer. The existing document text is immediately dimmed and the Header text box at the top of your document opens. A floating Header and Footer toolbar, like the one shown in Figure 3.2, also opens.

F I G U R E 3.2: Header and Footer view

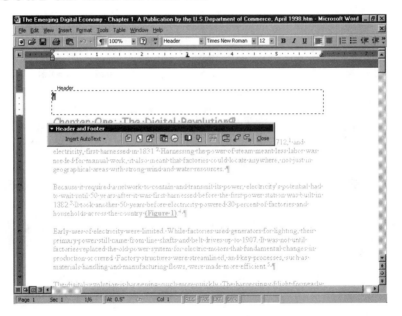

Enter the text you want to appear in the Header text box. Use the toolbar buttons to create and modify the headers and footers. See Table 3.1.

T A B L E 3.1: Header and Footer toolbar buttons

Button	Button Name	Placeholder
Insert AutoText ▾	Insert AutoText	Provides drop-down list of AutoText entries
	Insert Page Number	Inserts page number place-holder
	Insert Number of Pages	Inserts placeholder for total number of pages
	Format Page Number	Opens Page Number Format dialog box
	Insert Date	Inserts placeholder for date
	Insert Time	Inserts placeholder for time
	Page Setup	Opens Layout page of Page Setup dialog box
	Show/Hide Document Text	Makes document text visible or invisible while working with background
	Same As Previous	Makes header or footer the same as in previous section
	Switch Between Header and Footer	Changes view between Header and Footer text box
	Show Previous	Moves to previous section's header
	Show Next	Moves to next section's header

T A B L E 3.1: Header and Footer toolbar buttons *(continued)*

Button	Button Name	Placeholder
Close	Close Header and Footer	Closes Header and Footer view

Whether you are creating headers, footers, or both, the process is the same. Just move to the header or footer you want to add or edit. Use the Switch Between Header and Footer and Show Previous/Show Next buttons to navigate between the headers and footers in each section of your document.

TIP To suppress the header or footer on the first page, choose the Different First Page option from the Layout tab of the Page Setup dialog box and leave the header or footer blank.

Taking Care of Loose Ends

Before you print the final version of a document, you should clean up dangling words, bad line and page breaks, and extra spaces that detract from the appearance of your document. You can clean up these loose ends in three ways:

Hyphenation corrects spaces at the ends of lines where long words wrap to the beginning of the next line.

Nonbreaking Spaces keeps text strings together that shouldn't be broken over two lines.

Text Flow Options keeps paragraphs or lines of paragraphs together that currently break across two pages.

TIP Make sure you have done all your editing and formatting before attempting any of this final cleanup. When you add, delete, or reformat text, you have to clean up the document all over again.

Handling Line Breaks

Word includes options for automatically and manually hyphenating your documents. To have Word automatically hyphenate your document, choose Tools ➤ Language ➤ Hyphenation and click the Automatically Hyphenate Document check box:

TIP If you want to prevent a word or phrase that contains a hyphen (such as a phone number) from breaking at the end of a line, you can insert a *nonbreaking hyphen* by holding down Ctrl+Shift when you enter the hyphen. To enter an *optional hyphen*, a hyphen that breaks a word or a phrase at the designated place if it occurs at the end of a line, hold down Ctrl when you enter the hyphen.

Nonbreaking Spaces

Occasionally, you might have a text string, such as an address, that should not be separated at the end of a line. You can protect this string by inserting nonbreaking spaces instead of regular spaces within the text string. Similar to a nonbreaking hyphen, text connected with *nonbreaking spaces* will move to the next line rather then breaking between lines. To insert a non-breaking space, hold Ctrl and Shift when you press the spacebar.

Handling Page Breaks

Objective W2000E.1.2

Word 2000 offers a number of other ways to keep text together. One of these options, with the tacky name *Widow/Orphan Control*, is on by default. This feature prevents the first line of a paragraph from being left alone at the bottom of the page (an orphan) or the last line of a paragraph from appearing by itself at the top of a new page (a widow). You can turn

off Widow/Orphan Control in the Line and Page Breaks dialog box
(choose Format ➤ Paragraph ➤ Line and Page Breaks).

If you want to keep specific lines or paragraphs of text together, first select
the text and then open the dialog box.

Adjusting Line and Page Breaks

1. Choose Format ➤ Paragraph ➤ Line and Page Breaks to turn text
   flow options on or off for Widow/Orphan Control, Keep Lines
   Together, Keep with Next, and Page Break Before.

2. Press Ctrl+Shift+hyphen to insert a nonbreaking hyphen.

3. Press Ctrl+hyphen to insert an optional hyphen.

4. Press Ctrl+Shift+spacebar to insert a nonbreaking space.

Hands On

Objectives W2000.3.5, 3.9, 3.10, 3.16, E.1.2, and E.2.2

1. Open an existing document, or create a new document that is at least
   three pages long. Save the document before proceeding.

   a) Add a header that contains the name of the document and the
      date to all but the first page.

     b) Insert a centered page number. Do not number the first page.

     c) Save the document under a different name and then print it.

2. Manually hyphenate an existing document.

3. Create a footer for the odd pages and a different footer for the even pages of a document.

4. Modify the footers you created in Exercise 3 by adding the date to them.

5. Select a paragraph that has a page break in the middle of it. Set text flow options so the page does not break in the middle of the paragraph.

Working with Columns

Some kinds of information are most effectively presented in tabular or newspaper columns. Tabular parallel columns, discussed later in this chapter, display corresponding text in columns (like a phone book). With *newspaper columns*, text flows from the bottom of one column to the top of the next. If you create newsletters, flyers, reports, announcements, or other types of publications, you'll probably use Word's newspaper columns feature quite a bit.

Working with Newspaper Columns

Working with columns requires a little advance-design work. You'll find it is often easier to enter document text into a single column and then convert the text into multiple columns. Because of the space between the columns, one page of text takes up more than a page when poured into two or more columns. As a result, you may have to go back and edit text to get it to fit on a prescribed number of pages. However, by first focusing on your writing and then switching your attention to the design issues, you'll very likely end up with a higher quality product in the long run.

Entering and Editing Text in Columns

Objectives W2000.3.12 and E.2.7

To work with columns, switch to Print Layout view so you can actually see the columns as they will appear on the page. Although you can format columns in Normal view, you won't be able to see the results.

Creating Columns

1. To create columns from exisiting text, switch to Print Layout view. Select the text you want to change to columns.

2. Click the Columns button on the Standard toolbar and drag to select the number of columns you want.

   OR

1. To set up columns and then enter text, switch to Print Layout view.

2. Click the Columns button on the Standard toolbar and drag to select the number of columns you want.

3. Enter text into the column. To make equal columns, like those in Figure 3.3, move the insertion point to the end of the text and insert a continuous section break (Insert ➤ Break ➤ Continuous).

4. To enter a title that spans the columns, enter the title at the beginning of the first column. Select the title, click the Columns button, and select one column.

F I G U R E   3.3: Text in columns

Revising Column Structure

Objective W2000.3.13

Word provides you with several options for changing the number of columns in your document, the column width, and the white space in the gutter between columns.

If you decide you want to change the number of columns in your document, move the insertion point into the columns section, click the Columns button and drag to select the new number of columns. To revert to a single column, choose one column or switch to Normal view and delete the section breaks.

When you create columns with the Columns button, Word makes all the columns the same width. If you want columns of differing widths, drag the Move Column marker on the horizontal ruler.

To change the white space in the gutter between the columns, drag the Left and Right Margin markers on the inside of the columns.

Using the Columns Dialog Box

To establish columns of a specific width or to lock columns so they will remain equally wide, use the Columns dialog box (Format ➤ Columns), shown in Figure 3.4. Choose One, Two, or Three from the Presets options; the Equal Column Width check box will be selected automatically. Choose Left or Right from the Presets if you want two columns of unequal size. You can create up to 10 columns using the Number of Columns spin box. Enter the column width and the spacing between columns if you would like settings different from the defaults. Click the Line Between check box to have Word insert vertical lines between each of the columns.

F I G U R E 3.4: Columns dialog box

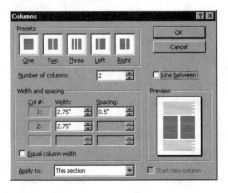

Keeping Text Together in Columns

All the tools you use to keep page text together, including nonbreaking spaces, nonbreaking hyphens, and Lines and Spacing options, work with columns. Word's Columns dialog box provides you with one other option for controlling where text breaks between columns. Move the insertion point to the beginning of the text you want to reposition in the next column and choose Format ➤ Columns to open the Columns dialog box. Change the Apply To control to This Point Forward and enable the Start New Column check box to insert an End of Section marker and move the text to the next column.

Restructuring Columns

1. To add or delete columns, click anywhere in the columns section of your document and click the Columns button. Drag to select the desired number of columns.

2. Drag the Move Column marker on the ruler to change column width and to move columns left or right.

3. Drag the Left or Right Margin markers on the ruler to change the white space between columns.

4. Open the Columns dialog box (choose Format ➤ Columns), shown in Figure 3.4, to create as many as 10 columns, to lock columns so they are of equal width, to insert a line between columns, or to enter exact measurements for column widths and spacing.

5. To move text into the next column, move the insertion point in front of the text you want to move. Open the Columns dialog box and choose This Point Forward in the Apply To control. Click the Start New Column check box to move the text to the next column.

Hands On

Objectives W2000.3.12, 3.13, and E.2.7

1. Open an existing document, or create a new document that contains several paragraphs of text.

    a) Format the text for two columns. Enter two paragraphs of text. Balance the column length by inserting a continuous section break.

b) Use the ruler to change the column widths, making the first column wider than the second.

c) Add a line between the columns.

d) Add a title that spans both columns. Save the document as Working with Columns.

e) Move the last sentence that begins in the first column to the second column by using Keeping Text Together options.

2. In the same document:

a) Change Working with Columns, or another document with columns, back to a single column. (You may have to delete additional section breaks—switch to Normal view to see them.)

b) Use the Presets in the Columns dialog box to change the text to three columns of equal width.

c) Add another paragraph of text to the end of the section.

Constructing High-Quality Tables

Although you can use tabs to present information in parallel columns, it is far easier to use Word's powerful Tables features. With tables, every block of text can be easily formatted, edited, deleted, and moved around without affecting the remainder of the text. Tables are one of the most versatile tools in the Word 2000 toolkit.

Creating and Revising Tables

Objective W2000.5.1

 You create tables in Word 2000 in three ways: using the Insert Table button, using the Insert Table dialog box, and using the Draw Table button.

To use the Insert Table button, click the button and drag the number of columns and rows you want in your table.

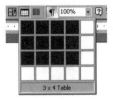

When you release the mouse button, a blank table appears in your document.

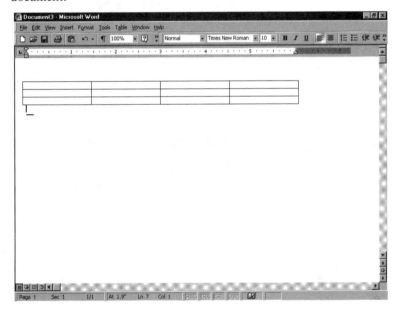

To create a table using the Insert Table dialog box, choose Table ➤ Insert ➤ Table. Enter the number of rows, columns, and column widths in the appropriate controls. When you create a table, it's easiest if you determine the number of columns you're going to need before you start. You can always add columns later, but it may mean changing the widths of the other columns to accommodate them. Adding rows, on the other hand, is as simple as pressing Tab at the end of a row. To create a table that is as wide as your page, leave the Fixed Column Width setting on Auto. When you've entered all the settings, click OK to create the table.

You can also draw a table exactly the way you want it to appear.

Clicking the Tables and Borders button on the Standard toolbar opens the Tables and Borders toolbar; the mouse pointer will change to a pencil. Drag the pencil to create a rectangle about the size of the table you want:

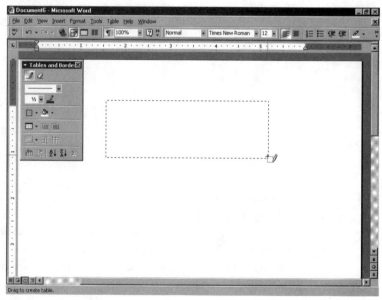

When you release the mouse button, the outside border of the table appears in your document. Use the pencil again to draw in column and row borders:

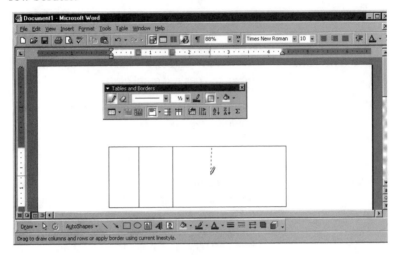

Entering and Editing Text

Once you have created a table, you enter text by clicking in any *cell* (the intersection of a column and row). Use the Tab key or the Right arrow key on the keyboard to move to the next cell to the right. Shift+Tab or the Left arrow key will move one cell to the left. The Up and Down arrow keys will move the insertion point to the cell below or above the current cell.

If you created your table by drawing it, click the Draw Table button on the Tables and Borders toolbar or close the toolbar to change the pointer back from a pencil to that old familiar I-beam so you can begin typing.

Table 3.2 shows how to select portions of a table.

T A B L E 3.2: Selecting in Tables

To Select	Action
A cell	Triple-click in the cell, or click the right-pointing, solid-black arrow inside a cell.

T A B L E 3.2:   Selecting in Tables *(continued)*

To Select	Action
A row	Move mouse to the left margin, point to the row, and click.
Multiple rows	Select the first row, hold down mouse button, and drag down the desired number of rows.
A column	Move the mouse above a column. It will change to a downward-pointing arrow. Click. OR Hold down the Alt key and click the column.
Multiple columns	Select the first column, hold down the mouse button, and drag the desired number of columns. OR For contiguous columns, select the first column (any method), and then hold down Shift and select the last column (any method).
Entire table	Choose Table ➤ Select Table. OR Hold down the Alt key and double-click. OR Click the Move icon (the 4-headed arrow) that appears to the upper right of a table when you click anywhere inside it.

Formatting Text in Tables

Each table cell can be formatted separately. Whatever you can do to a paragraph, you can do to the text within a cell. Use the Standard toolbar or the Format menu to apply fonts, font effects, alignment, bullets and numbering, and indents and spacing to the text in a table.

The Tables and Borders toolbar also provides some additional formatting options unique to tables.

The default alignment is the top left of the cell. Click the drop-down arrow next to the alignment button on the Tables and Borders toolbar to see other choices. Click one of the nine alignment options to place text exactly where you want it in a cell.

Rotating Text in Tables

Objective W2000.5.5

When you really want to draw attention to your text, rotate it so it is no longer running in the traditional direction across the page. With Word's Text Direction feature, you can rotate text in a table so it runs vertically, facing either right or left. Select the cell or group of cells that contain the text you want to rotate.

Then click the Change Text Direction button on the Tables and Borders toolbar. The button is a toggle button, which means the first click rotates the text so it is facing left, the second click flips it so it faces right, and the third click returns it to the tried-and-true horizontal.

As the text rotates, so do some of the buttons on the Formatting and Tables and Borders toolbars. The alignment buttons, Numbering, Bullets, and Text Direction all change to match the rotation of the text:

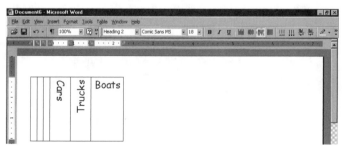

Even the I-beam and the insertion point rotate, so editing can be a little disconcerting at first, but it's technically no different from horizontal editing. The main thing to remember is that you have to drag the mouse vertically to select text. Once you've gotten the hang of that, you're all set.

Entering, Editing, and Positioning Text in Tables

1. Click any cell and begin typing. Use the Tab key to move one cell to the right, Shift+Tab to move to the left, and arrow keys to move up and down or left and right.

2. Apply any character or paragraph formatting options to the text. Each cell is treated as a paragraph.

3. Click one of the alignment buttons on the Tables and Borders toolbar to reposition text within a cell.

4. Click the Change Text Direction button on the Tables and Borders toolbar to rotate text vertically.

Modifying Table Structure

You can easily modify tables. You can add or delete rows and columns, change column and row widths, and merge and split cells without upsetting the rest of the table text.

Adding and Deleting Rows and Columns

Objective W2000.5.3

To add a row at the end of a table, simply move to the last cell in the table and press Tab. If you want to insert rows in the middle of the table, select the number of rows you want to insert and choose Table ➤ Insert ➤ Rows Above or Table ➤ Insert ➤ Rows Below, or right-click and choose Insert Rows from the shortcut menu. Word will insert the rows ahead of the first selected row.

To delete rows, select the rows you want to delete. Choose Table ➤ Delete ➤ Rows, or right-click and choose Delete Rows from the shortcut menu. If you select a cell rather than an entire row, choose Table ➤ Delete ➤ Cells, which opens the Delete Cells dialog box:

You can choose to delete the current cell and shift the remaining cells left or up. If you want to delete a whole row or column, choose Delete Entire Row or Delete Entire Column.

Inserting columns works the same way as inserting rows. New rows and new columns are the same width as the ones you select to create them, so you may have to adjust the widths of newly-inserted columns if they no longer fit the width of the page.

TIP To insert a column at the end of a table, click the last column and then choose Table ➤ Insert ➤ Columns to the Right. To insert a column at the beginning of the table, click the first column, and then choose Table ➤ Insert ➤ Columns to the Left.

Changing Column and Cell Widths

Objective W2000.5.4

The easiest way to adjust a column or a row is to move the insertion point to the border between the row or column. The insertion point will change to a double-headed arrow, allowing you to drag the border in either direction:

1	2	3	4	5
A	B	C	D	E
F	G	H	I	J
K	L	M	O	P
Q	R	S	T	U
V	W	X	Y	Z

If you drag with a cell selected, you're only changing the width for that cell. To be certain, you can, of course, select the entire column or row before dragging.

At times you may want to make all the columns the same width or all rows the same height (for example, when creating a calendar). Select the columns or rows you want to be the same width or height and choose Table ➤ AutoFit ➤ Distribute Columns Evenly or Table ➤ AutoFit ➤ Distribute Rows Evenly, and Word will do the work for you. The Tables and Borders toolbar also has buttons to distribute rows and columns evenly.

You can make another quick adjustment after you enter all the text in your table. Select the columns you want to adjust and choose Table ➤ AutoFit ➤ AutoFit to Contents to automatically adjust the width of the columns to the widest entry.

You can also enter exact height and width measurements for columns and rows. Choose Table ➤ Table Properties to open the Table Properties dialog box. To adjust the width of a column, select the Column tab, as shown in Figure 3.5, and change the measurement in the Preferred Width spin box. Click the Previous Column or Next Column button to adjust the measurement of the previous or next column.

FIGURE 3.5: The Table Properties dialog box, with the Column tab selected

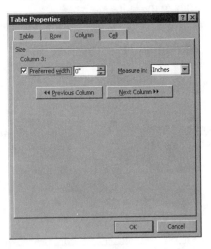

To adjust the height of a row, select the Row tab in the Table Properties dialog box, as shown in Figure 3.6, and change the measurement in the Specify Height spin box.

The Row tab offers some other important options. In the Row Height Is box, select At Least if you want the rows to maintain a minimum height regardless of what is in them. Select Exactly when you want to designate a row height that doesn't change. This is useful when you are creating calendars, for example, and you want the row height to stay the same regardless of the contents.

Click the Previous Row or Next Row button to adjust the height and other characteristics of the previous or next row.

FIGURE 3.6: The Table Properties dialog box, with the Row tab selected

Merging and Splitting Cells

Objective W2000.5.4

It doesn't take much work with tables to discover that you don't want the same number of cells in every row or column. You might want to put a title in a single cell that spans the top of the table. Or you might be creating a form and want fewer columns for the totals. When you want to make one cell from two or more cells, you *merge* the cells. *Split* cells to separate a single cell into multiple cells.

 To merge cells, simply select the cells you want to merge and Choose Tables ➤ Merge Cells, or click the Merge Cells button on the Tables and Borders toolbar.

 If you prefer the visual approach, you can use the Eraser on the Tables and Borders toolbar to erase the border between cells you want to merge. Drag the Eraser horizontally to merge rows or vertically to merge columns.

Use the Draw Table pencil from the Tables and Borders toolbar to split cells,

 or choose Table ➤ Split Cells or click the Split Cells button to open the Split Cells dialog box:

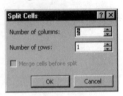

Use the dialog box's spin box controls to enter the number of columns and rows you would like to divide the selected cell(s) into. Enable the Merge Cells Before Split check box if you want to apply the new row and column settings to several selected cells. This is one way to quickly reconfigure your table. For example, if you selected a 3×3 table, you could convert it to a 4×3 table by entering 4 columns, 3 rows in the Split Cells dialog box and enabling the Merge Cells Before Split feature. You can wind up with a real mess if you've already entered text in your table, however. It's best to reserve this feature for empty tables that need reconfiguring.

Modifying Table Structure

1. Insert rows at the end of a table by clicking in the last cell and pressing Tab. Insert rows in the middle of the table by selecting the number of rows you want to insert and choosing Table ➤ Insert ➤ Rows Above or Table ➤ Insert ➤ Rows Below.

2. Delete rows by selecting the rows you want to delete and choosing Table ➤ Delete ➤ Rows.

3. Insert columns by selecting the number of columns you want to insert and selecting Table ➤ Insert ➤ Columns to the Left or Table ➤ Insert ➤ Columns to the Right.

4. Change the width of columns by pointing to the cell border and dragging the border with the column-adjustment pointer.

5. Merge cells by selecting the cells you want to merge and choosing Table ➤ Merge Cells or by clicking the Merge Cells button.

Modifying Table Structure *(continued)*

6. Split cells by dragging the Draw Table button in the cell you want to split. You can also select a cell and click the Split Cells button on the Tables and Borders toolbar if you want to enter the number of rows and columns in the Split Cells dialog box.

Formatting Tables

Before you print your table, you might want to put some finishing touches on it to give it that polished, professional look. Word 2000 offers both automatic and manual table formatting options to add and remove borders, change border types, and add colors and shading.

Using AutoFormat

AutoFormat provides you with a number of formats you can apply in one easy step. Click anywhere in your table and choose Table ➤ Table Auto-Format to open the Table AutoFormat dialog box shown in Figure 3.7.

F I G U R E   3.7: Table AutoFormat dialog box

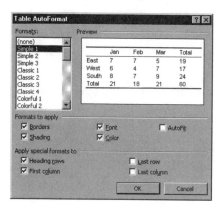

AutoFormat applies borders, shading, fonts, and colors. Most of the formats include special formatting for the header row, last row, and first and last columns since these often contain titles or summary information. Turn checkmarks on or off to indicate which formatting options you want to apply. Choosing any of the formats will give you a preview of the format. Click OK when you want to apply the selected format to your table.

If you're not satisfied, click Undo, or choose Table ➤ AutoFormat again and select a different format. To remove an AutoFormat, open the Table AutoFormat dialog box and choose None from the scroll list.

Adding Your Own Borders and Shading

Objective W2000.5.2

You don't have to settle for the predesigned AutoFormats. You can adjust AutoFormats manually or start from scratch, whichever you prefer. Either way, you'll want to turn on the Tables and Borders toolbar before you begin formatting.

The Line Style, Line Weight, and Border Color buttons all relate to the cell borders. Click the drop-down arrow next to Line Style or Line Weight to select from the list of choices available. Clicking the Border Color button opens a color menu. Select a color and use the pencil pointer to draw over borders you want to color. Make sure you draw over the entire length of the border, or the color will not be applied. All three buttons are dynamic, which means your most recent choice appears on the button to make it easy to reapply.

To apply a border, select the cells you want to apply a border to, select the Line Style, Line Weight, and Border Color you want to apply, and click the Borders button to open a drop-down menu:

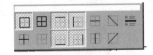

Click the type of border you want to apply.

 Click the Shading Color button down arrow to open a menu of shading colors, including various shades of gray. If you are applying a lot of different borders and shading to your table, you can pull the menus off the toolbar so they float on the surface of your document:

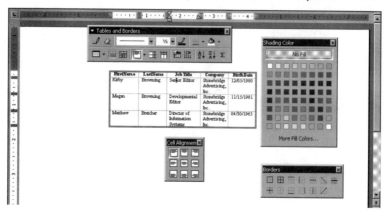

You can then apply as many borders or shades as you want without having to open the menus each time. To float the menus, click the drop-down arrow to open the menu. Point to the gray bar at the top of the menu; the bar will turn the same color as your Windows title bars. Drag the menu into the document. When you're finished with the menu, just click its Close button.

Objectives W2000.2.4, E.1.1, and E.2.1

Borders and Shading are not limited to use in tables. You can apply to any paragraph of text the same skills you just learned. Just select one or more paragraphs and click the Tables and Borders button, or choose Format ➤ Borders and Shading.

To apply a border to the entire page or a section of a document, click the Page Borders tab. Choose the type of border you want to apply and click the Apply To down arrow to specify the whole document or section. Click the Art button to add fancy graphic borders to the page.

TIP If you're having trouble getting a page border to print correctly, click the Options button on the Page Borders tab of the Borders and Shading dialog box and adjust the margins accordingly

---

Centering Tables Horizontally

If you've adjusted the column widths in your table, it may no longer extend across the entire width of the page. In Word 2000, you can center the table between the left and right margins by selecting the entire table and clicking the Center button on the Formatting toolbar.

Performing Calculations in a Word Table

Objective W2000E.3.2

There will almost certainly be times when you want to add, multiply, average, or otherwise calculate numbers in a table. Word 2000 provides the tools necessary to "do the math!" Figure 3.8 shows an example of a table with a simple sum.

F I G U R E 3.8: Table with a Sum

Creekside Upper Elementary School Spring T-shirt Order

Teacher	Small	Medium	Large	Total
Bailey	12	3	2	17
Holt	8	11	7	26
Middleton	8	8	6	22
Turner	4	7	7	18

Including Calculations in a Word Table

1. Position the insertion point in the cell where you want the result to appear.

2. Click Table ➤ Formula.

3. Modify the fields in the Formula dialog box to reflect the actual calculation you want to perform. For example, if the Formula field is set to =SUM(ABOVE) and you want to sum the numbers to the left (as we did in Figure 3.9), simply select "ABOVE" and overtype it with "LEFT."

4. If you want a function other than SUM, use the Paste Function drop-down list to choose another such as AVERAGE, COUNT, or IF.

Including Calculations in a Word Table *(continued)*

5. Enter a format for the numbers in the Number Format box. For example, to display two non-significant zeros behind the decimal point (i.e., 22 displays as 22.00) choose 0.00 from the list.

6. Repeat the procedure for each cell that requires a calculation. If you change the numbers included in the formula, select the calculated field and press F9 to update it.

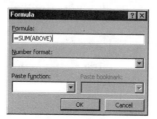

TIP   Although it is possible to include calculations in Word tables, the Word Help file on formulas suggests that if you know how to use Excel, embedding all or part of a worksheet is often easier than using formulas in a Word table. We certainly agree. To learn more about embedding an Excel worksheet, see Chapter 5.

Hands On

Objectives W2000.5.1, 5.2, 5.3, 5.4, 5.5, and E3.2.

1. Open a new document:

    a) Change the Page Orientation to Landscape. Using the Draw Table feature, insert a seven-column, six-row table to create a calendar for the current month.

    b) Select the columns and click Distribute Columns Evenly. Enter the names of the days of the week in the first row of the table. Center the day names horizontally and vertically. Change the font and font size as appropriate.

c) Insert a new row at the top of the table. Merge the cells in the row and enter the current month and year using a large font size. Center the text vertically and horizontally. Shade the row.

d) Enter and right-align dates for the month in the appropriate cells of the table.

e) Drag the last row so it is just above the bottom margin. Select the date rows and choose Distribute Rows Evenly to make them all the same size.

f) Change the outside border to a thicker, more decorative border. Change the bottom border under the title to a different border type.

g) Identify two important dates in the month and shade them.

h) Insert a document title and an introductory paragraph of text *above* the table. (Press Ctrl+Home to move to the top of the document and press Enter to create blank lines above the table.) Insert a border around the title and apply shading to it.

i) Experiment with rotating text in your table.

2. Duplicate the table shown in Figure 3.9, including its formulas. Or create a table that shows information related to a project you are working on. Use Borders and Shading to make the table attractive and at least one formula to perform a calculation.

Working Smarter with Word

One of the things computers are supposed to prevent is repeating the same tasks over and over again, and Word 2000 does its share of prevention. Learning to use styles and templates may take a bit of practice, but once they become part of your routine, you'll wonder how you lived without them.

You've Got Style

Word's Styles feature lets you save existing formats and apply them to other text. Styles can include fonts, sizes, font attributes, alignment, character spacing, paragraph spacing, bullets and numbering, borders, indenting, and just about any other formatting you can think of. Once you've created a style, all you have to do to apply the style is select it from a list. But the major benefit of styles is that if you change a style, all the text using that style is automatically changed, too—much easier than adjusting the font size on 25 subheadings.

Getting to Know Styles

Objective W2000.3.15

When you open a new Word document, at the beginning of the Formatting toolbar you'll find a list of default styles available for your use:

To use any of the default styles, click the drop-down arrow next to Normal and select the style you want to apply. You can apply a style before entering text, or you can apply it to selected text. You'll notice the items on the list are formatted to show the style.

Applying Styles

1. Click the Styles drop-down arrow on the Formatting toolbar and choose a style from the list.

2. To apply a style to existing text, select the text and then choose the style.

TIP To automatically apply heading styles 1 through 9 as you are creating a document, choose Tools ➤ AutoCorrect to open the AutoCorrect dialog box. Click the AutoFormat As You Type tab, and in the Apply As You Type section, click the Headings check box. To automatically apply heading styles 1 through 9 when AutoFormatting a document, click the AutoFormat tab in the AutoCorrect dialog box, and in the Apply section, click the Headings check box.

A Style All Your Own

Objective W2000E.2.4

Once you start working with styles, it won't be long before you're dissatisfied with the basic selection and want to create your own styles. Not a problem. Simply format a paragraph the way you would like the style to appear and click in the Style text box. Type the name of your style and press Enter. The newly created style in Figure 3.9 is 26-pt. bold, italic, Comic Sans MS, centered, with a shadow border.

F I G U R E 3.9: A newly created style

Now when you look at the drop-down list, the new style appears on the list and illustrates what it looks like:

To apply the style to other text, select the text and select the style from the list.

Redefining Styles

After you've created and applied a style, you may decide that you don't like the font or you need some extra spacing between paragraphs. It's in situations like this that styles really shine. You can redefine the style, and it will automatically change all the text formatted in that style throughout the entire document. To change a style, select a paragraph that uses the style and make the desired changes. While the paragraph is still selected, click in the Styles text box, and rather than typing in a new name, just press Enter. The Modify Style dialog box appears, which gives you two choices: Do you want to update the style to reflect the changes you made to this selection, or do you want to cancel the changes you made and reapply the prior formatting?

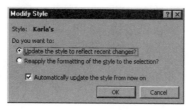

This dialog box also allows you to automatically update the style if you make future changes to text where the style is applied. It's safer to ignore this check box because you're not warned when your formatting changes will affect a style.

Some styles include spacing before or after a paragraph. If you want to change the amount of spacing included in a style, select a sample paragraph, choose Format ➤ Paragraph, and on the Indents and Spacing page, adjust Spacing Before and After. When you've made the changes, redefine the style.

If you create a style you would like to have available whenever you create documents, you can assign the style to the Normal template, which opens every time you create a new blank document. Choose Format ➤ Style, select the style from the list, and choose Modify. Click the Add to Template check box. Now every time you create a new blank document, your style will be available.

Creating and Redefining Styles

1. Format a paragraph with the options you would like contained in the style.

2. Click in the Style text box and type a name for the new style; press Enter.

3. Select another paragraph and choose the new style from the drop-down list.

4. To redefine a style, select a paragraph and change the formatting. Click in the Style text box and press Enter.

5. Choose Update the Style to Reflect Recent Changes.

To delete a style from the Normal template, choose Format ➤ Style, select the style from the list and choose Organizer to open the Style Organizer. Choose the style or styles in the To NORMAL.DOT list and click the Delete button, then choose Yes; to delete several selected styles without further prompting, click Yes to All. Click Close to close the Style Organizer. Remember, though, that any and all documents based on the style will be reformatted to another style, so you should never delete a style that has been used in existing documents.

NOTE   You cannot delete any of Word's built-in styles.

Hands On

Objectives W2000.3.15 and E.2.4

1. Open an existing document that contains a title and several subheadings. If you'd prefer to create a new document, enter a title at the top of the document, enter a heading, and type a paragraph.

   a) Enter at least two more paragraphs, including headings above each one.

   b) Select the title and apply the Heading 1 style to it.

c) Select the first heading and apply the Heading 2 style. Use the Format Painter to apply the Heading 2 style to other similar headings (see Chapter 2 for information about the Format Painter).

d) If you have subheadings, apply the Heading 3 style to them.

e) Redefine the Heading 2 style, using a different font and other formatting options and update the style to reflect these changes.

f) Create a new paragraph style for the body text of your document.

g) Apply the new style to each of the body text paragraphs.

Creating Outlines in Word

You may remember an outline as that horrible thing you had create in school before your teacher would accept an assigned paper. Just trying to figure out which Roman numeral came next could be enough to spoil a good topic. You'll be happy to know that's not the kind of outline we're talking about here. In Word 2000, you can use heading styles (see the previous section) to view the major topics covered in your document—without having to scroll through pages and pages of text. You can collapse and expand heading levels to see more or less of your document at one time, making it a lot easier to ensure you've covered the essential subject matter. You can even print a collapsed outline of your completed document to use as a summary.

Creating an Outline

When you create an outline in Word 2000, you create the document's headings and subheadings in Outline view. After the outline is finished, you enter body text in Normal, Print Layout, or Web Layout view. If you're starting a new document, click the Outline View button on the horizontal scroll bar. The Outlining toolbar appears and the default style is set to Heading 1. To begin the outline, enter your first heading and press Enter. You can choose to enter all your first-level headings and then go back and enter lower level headings, or you can switch back and forth between them. Heading 1 does not actually refer to the first heading but to the first *level* of headings. You can have several level-1 headings in your document. To move down a level to Heading 2, press Tab. There are nine outlining heading levels you can use, as shown in Figure 3.10. If you want to change to a higher heading level, press Shift+Tab.

FIGURE 3.10: Outlining heading levels

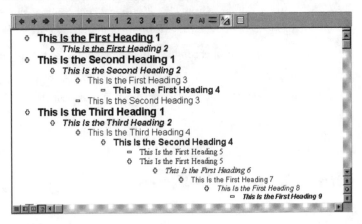

Promoting and Demoting Headings

When you want to change the level of an existing heading, you *promote* or *demote* it to move it to a higher or lower level. Select the heading as you would select a line. If you'd like to promote or demote a heading and any subheadings underneath it, point to the *outline symbol* (plus, minus, or square) in front of the heading, and click using the four-headed arrow (a plus means a heading has subheadings; a minus means that it does not) to select the entire section.

With the text selected, click the Promote or Demote button on the Outlining toolbar.

 You can demote headings to body text by clicking the Demote to Body Text button.

Viewing and Printing Selected Levels

Once you have entered your outline, you can display at one time as many levels as you would like. Click any of the seven Show Heading buttons on the Outlining toolbar to *collapse* the outline, which, in effect, hides all lower levels. For example, if you click Show Heading 3, headings 4 and above and body text will not be displayed.

Creating an Outline

1. Click the Outline View button to switch to Outline view.

2. Enter a level-one heading (Heading 1). Press Enter.

3. Press Tab to move to a lower heading level; press Shift+Tab to return to a higher level.

4. Select a single heading by clicking the left margin; select a whole section by clicking the plus or minus sign in front of the section.

5. To promote and demote selected text, click the Promote and Demote buttons.

When some outline levels aren't displayed, the squiggly line tells you there are hidden levels:

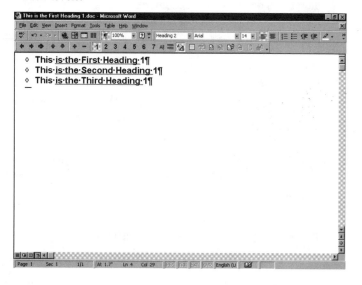

 Click the All button to *expand* the outline and see all levels again.

If you want to focus on a particular point, you can collapse lower levels and then expand just the one you want to see. Click the Show Heading 1 button to collapse the outline. Move the mouse pointer to the left margin and select the heading you want to expand.

Click the Expand button to expand one level at a time, or double-click the plus sign next to the heading to expand all levels in the section.

 Click the Collapse button to collapse one level at a time.

One of the great things about Outline view is that you can print the entire outline or any portion of it. Collapse or expand the outline so it shows just what you want to print, and then click the Print button. Print Preview will still show the entire outline. Don't worry about it. Only the expanded sections and headings will actually print.

TIP   Heading styles are directly supported in Outline view. Even if you didn't originally create a document in Outline view, as long as you used heading styles you can use the outlining features.

After you've created your outline, switch to Normal, Web Layout, or Print Layout view and enter body text under each heading, as shown in Figure 3.11. Just click to the right of the heading you want to write about, press Enter, and type the text. If you decide you are not satisfied with the outline, you can switch back to Outline view at any time and rearrange it.

Viewing and Printing Selected Portions of an Outline

1. Click any of the Show Heading buttons to hide headings below that level.

2. Click Show All to see the entire document.

3. Double-click the outline symbol to expand or collapse a section.

4. To print an outline, expand or collapse as desired and click Print.

Navigating with the Document Map

You can use the Document Map feature to navigate through a long document with relative ease, no matter what view you are in. Choose View ➤ Document Map in any view to open a frame, like the one shown in Figure 3.12, which contains all the headings. Just click a heading to move to that section.

F I G U R E 3.11: Entering body text in Print Layout view

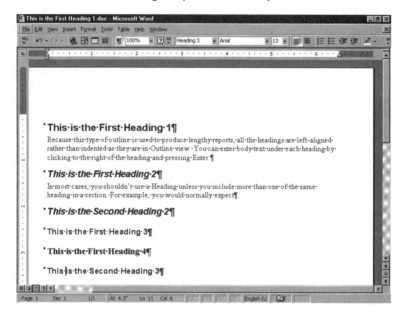

F I G U R E 3.12: Navigating with the Document Map

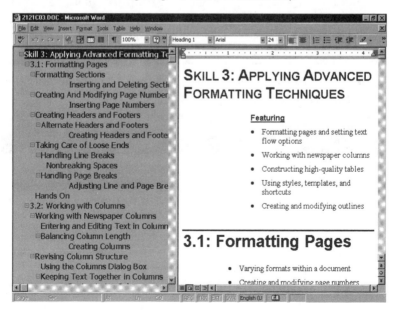

Unlike Outlining, the Document Map doesn't affect printing, so you can't use it to print parts of the document.

Modifying an Outline

Not only can you collapse and expand an outline, you can select a section of the outline and move it to another location. In Outline view, click the plus sign in front of the section, then drag it toward its new location. A horizontal line will appear. Drag-and-drop the line to move the section.

  You can use the Move Up and Move Down buttons on the Outlining toolbar, but make sure you click the button enough times to drop the section into the right spot. It's easy to rearrange your document in ways that you didn't anticipate—another reason that it's always a good idea to save before major rearranging.

Numbering an Outline

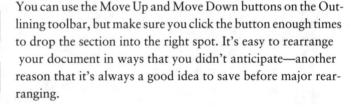

Objective W2000.2.7

Numbering headings in an outline is a snap! Just select the outline and click Format ➤ Bullets and Numbering to open the Bullets and Numbering dialog box. Click the Outline Numbered tab and select one of the choices for Headings or click Customize to create your own.

NOTE   See Chapter 2 for additional information about customized bulleted and numbered lists.

Modifying an Outline

1. Select the section you want to move by clicking its outline symbol.

2. Drag the section to its new location and drop it when the horizontal line is where you want the text.

3. Apply numbering to your outline by selecting it and clicking Format ➤ Bullets and Numbering. On the Outline Numbered tab, select a style that supports headings or click Customize to create your own.

Hands On

1. Create an outline on any topic with several heading levels similar to the one shown in Figure 3.11, or open a document that includes heading levels and switch to Outline view.
2. Collapse the outline to show only Heading 1.
3. Double-click an outline symbol to expand the subordinate text.
4. Demote two headings on the outline. Promote them back again or promote two other headings.
5. Expand the entire outline.
6. Switch to Normal view and enter body text under at least two of the headings.
7. Turn on the Document Map and navigate through your document.
8. Switch back to Outline view and move one heading and its subordinate text to another location.
9. Number your outline.

Using Templates

Objective W2000.4.7

Every document is based on a template. A *template* is a collection of document formatting options and content that is available when you create a new document. (The Normal, or standard, template also includes your AutoText entries, macros, toolbars, custom menu settings, and shortcut keys.) To help make your work easier, Word 2000 includes additional templates for preformatted documents and template *wizards* that walk you through a series of steps to customize a preformatted document.

When you choose File ➤ New from within Word or New Office Document from the Windows Start menu, you are presented with a choice of templates. Figure 3.13 shows the Letters & Faxes page of the New dialog box within Word. The available templates list depends on how Word was installed and whether any new templates have been created on your computer.

FIGURE 3.13: Letters & Faxes tab of the New dialog box

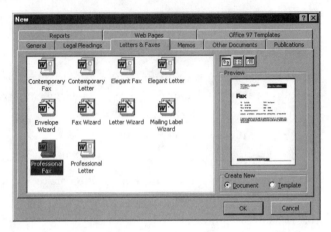

Any file with a .dot extension is a document template. Selections with .wiz are template wizards. Select any template to see a preview in the Preview window. (Templates created by other users often can't be previewed.) When you have selected a template you want to use, click OK.

Templates include placeholders where you can insert your text. They also generally include instructions to help you use the template. In the template shown in Figure 3.14, you can insert personalized text and then resave the template, so you can use it again without reentering your company or personal information.

When you save a document created from a template, you must give it a name just like any other new document. If you want to re-use the revised document as a template for future documents, or if you've created a document from scratch that you want to use as a template, click the Save As Type drop-down arrow in the Save As dialog box and choose Document Template (*.dot):

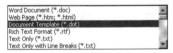

Selecting Document Template opens the Templates folder. If you wish, you can save your template in one of the existing folders. Enter a descriptive name for your template in the File Name control and save the template. Your template will now appear in the File ➤ New dialog box under the appropriate category or the General tab.

F I G U R E 3.14: Professional Memo template

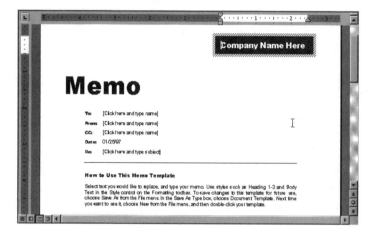

Setting a Default File Location for Workgroup Templates

Objective W2000E.7.5

Workgroup templates are templates that are shared by your entire workgroup. Your network administrator should create the workgroup folder and control what templates are saved there. If a workgroup templates folder is available on your network, you can identify the default file location so you can access the shared templates.

Setting the Default File Location for Workgroup Templates

1. Choose Tools ➤ Options and click the File Locations tab.

2. Select Workgroup Templates and click the Modify button.

3. Browse to the correct file location given to you by your workgroup administrator and when you find it, click OK.

4. Click Close to save the workgroup templates location.

WARNING If you are saving a regular document and the Save As dialog box *forces* you to save the document as a template, you may have a version of a Word macro virus on your system. You should immediately run a virus scan using virus protection software that can detect the Word Concept and other macro viruses. Visit the Microsoft Web site at http://www.microsoft.com for more information about macro viruses.

Using Wizards

Objective W2000.4.5

Wizards are helpful guides that walk you step-by-step through the process of creating a document. Click File ➤ New to see the wizards (and templates) in the New dialog box shown in Figure 3.15. Select a wizard and click OK. Figure 3.16 shows the first step of the Memo wizard.

F I G U R E 3.15: First step of the Memo wizard

The Start step of any wizard lists the steps you will follow in a vertical list on the left and briefly describes the purpose of the wizard below the title on the right. Your job is to read the instructions at each step, make choices as they are offered, and click Next to proceed. Some wizard steps, like the one shown in Figure 3.16, require that you type information that will be placed in your document later. You can return to any step of the Wizard and change your options by clicking the Back button. When you're through with all the steps, click Finish and Word incorporates your choices into a document. You may have further editing to do once the document is on screen. Proceed as you would with any Word document, saving the changes when you're done.

F I G U R E 3.16: Heading Fields step of the Memo Wizard

Hands On

Objectives W2000.4.5 and 4.7

1. Create a fax cover sheet using one of the templates in the New dialog box.

   a) Overwrite the placeholders with your own text.

   b) Print the document if you wish.

   c) Delete all the information you typed except for your company information, and then save the cover sheet as a template.

2. Use the Memo wizard or another wizard to create a document you can use for a project you're working on. Edit and save the document as necessary once the wizard finishes.

CHAPTER

4

Working with Complex Documents

So you've got a stack of 400 catalogs that need mailing labels? Time to redo the human resources manual? Or perhaps you just want to send a similar memo to 12 of your 15 department heads. Word 2000 can help!

Whether the job is large or small, increasing your Word 2000 expertise is a sure way to know you're making the best use of your precious time and resources. Effectively using advanced features such as mail merge, table of contents, and workgroup editing will set you apart from the crowd and give you a storehouse of tools to organize even the most unmanageable project.

Managing Data in Word

Word is more than just a word processor, it is a tool for managing information. Using Word, you can enter, sort, and search through lists of data: names, addresses, and items in an inventory. You can merge data lists with other Word documents and print labels, envelopes, and form letters. In this section, you will learn to create and sort lists. You'll also learn how to produce form letters, labels, and other merged documents in the "Creating Customized Merge Documents" section.

Understanding Mail Merge

The ability to store lists—personal or business contacts, members of groups or clubs, videotapes, CDs, or books—puts extra power in your hands. Using Word, you can access data stored in:

- a file created using Word
- a file created with other Microsoft Office products
- an external file created using other software

The file that contains a list of information is called a *data source*. (The term *database* also refers to this kind of file.) You can easily sort the information in the data source or use the data source to create labels or envelopes. Create a *main document* that refers to the information in the data source, and you can *merge* the main document with the data source to create personalized letters, labels, or other documents. In summary, you'll need two files to complete a merge: the data source and the main merge document.

Creating a New Data Source in Word

Objective W2000E.5.2

The Mail Merge Helper helps you create data sources and produce merged documents. Before you can get to the step where you're setting up the data, however, you have to do some preliminary work. Open the Mail Merge Helper by choosing Tools ➤ Mail Merge. Begin by clicking the Create button (see Figure 4.1) and selecting the type of document you will create using your data source. Although Word asks you to specify a type of document, your choice at this point doesn't preclude creating another type of main document later.

F I G U R E 4.1: The Mail Merge Helper

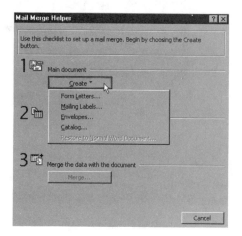

After you select the type of main document you want to create, Word asks if you want to use the active (open) document or a new document for your main document.

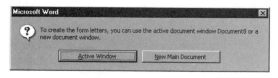

Choose Active Window if the open document is blank or if you've already opened a previously saved document to modify it for use with this merge; if you have any other document open, choose New Main Document.

Now that Word has the preliminary information it needs for the merge, you can proceed to the data step. Click the Get Data button, and then choose Create Data Source from the list to open the Create Data Source dialog box. (The other Get Data options are discussed later in the chapter.) Your goal at this step is to choose the categories for your data. The Create Data Source dialog box, shown in Figure 4.2, comes with a list of *field names* (categories of data) commonly used in mail merges. Scroll the list to find field names you may want to use.

F I G U R E 4.2: Create Data Source dialog box

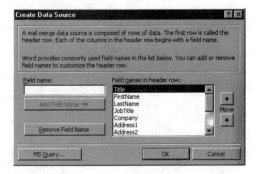

Field names must:

- Be unique—no two fields can have the same name.

- Have less than 40 characters—Word doesn't support larger field names but other programs, like Excel, do.

- Begin with a letter rather than a number—`Supervisor1` and `Supervisor2` are OK; `1Supervisor` and `2Supervisor` are not.

Field names must not:

- Contain spaces—you can separate words with an underscore (`First_Name`), but we suggest omitting the underscore and simply capitalizing the first letter of each word (`FirstName`)

- Contain any characters that you can't put in filenames, such as periods, commas, colons, semicolons, slashes, and backslashes—that means you can't use Audit3/15/2000, but you can use Audit3_15_ 2000 or Audit03152000.

The way you set up your data source can have lasting consequences, so it's a good idea to put some thought into it at the start. Chances are you'll want to use this data to create many different types of main documents. If you create one field called "Name," you probably won't run into any problems using the data for mailing labels. But what if you want to send a letter? You can never begin the letter with "Dear Mr. Hadley" or "Dear Susan" if you've combined first and last name data into one field.

Similarly, you can never sort your mailing labels by zip code if you've entered city, state, and zip into one field. In general, you'll want to enter data into the smallest discrete units that make sense. StreetAddress can usually include the whole field, 123 Ridge Road, unless you do mailings where you determine recipients by their street names. (Example: Your data contains addresses for everyone in Chesterfield Township, but you want to mail *only* to people who live on Ridge Road.) And don't forget fields you might want later like CourtesyTitle (Mr., Mrs., Ms.), Suffix (Jr., Sr., III), and JobTitle (Account Executive, Vice President of Human Resources). If you are creating several data source files, it's helpful to use the same field names in each data source. For example, if you use First-Name in one data source, don't use FNAME or First in other source files. If you use the same field names, you'll often be able to use the same main documents with different data source files, rather than creating new main documents.

In the Create Data Source dialog box, all the field names in the list are included in the data source by default. To remove a field name from the list, select it, then click the Remove Field Name button. To add a field name to the list, type the name in the Field Name control, and click the Add Field Name button. If you enter an illegal field name (for example, a name that contains a space or that already appears on the list), the Add Field Name button will be disabled to prevent you from adding the illegal name. Use the Move Up and Move Down buttons to the right of the fields list to arrange the field names in the order you'll be using to enter the actual data.

After you enter and arrange all the field names, click OK. You will be prompted to save the data source file. When you save the file, Word will remind you that the file contains no records and will ask whether you want to edit the data source or edit the main document. At this point, you can begin entering information in the data source file by choosing Edit the Data Source.

TIP When you save a data source file, it's a good idea to name the document so that it is easily identifiable as a data source file. You might want to begin all your data source filenames with Data: for example, Data-Employees.

Entering Records

Click the Edit Data Source button to open the Data Form dialog box (Figure 4.3). Enter the information for each field in your first record. When you are ready to enter another record, click the Add New button or press Enter. You can add other records any time you need to, so you don't have to enter all 10,000 employees right now, but can add as many as you wish.

F I G U R E 4.3: Data Form dialog box to enter records

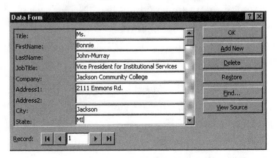

When you are finished, you can view all the records by clicking the View Source button. If you have 31 or fewer field names, Word places your document in a table. With 32 or more field names, the data source is displayed in columnar form.

Creating and Entering Records in a Data Source File

1. Choose Tools ➤ Mail Merge.

2. Choose Create and select a type of main document.

3. Indicate whether you want to use the active window as the main document or to create a new document.

4. Click Get Data, and then choose Create Data Source.

5. Review the list of suggested field names in the Create Data Source dialog box; delete field names you don't want.

6. Add new field names by entering them in the Field Name text box and clicking Add Field Name.

7. Use the Move arrows to arrange your fields in the desired order.

8. Click OK when you are finished entering field names and are ready to save the file.

9. Enter a filename for the data source file in the Save As dialog box. Click Save.

10. To begin entering data, choose Edit Data Source when the Option dialog box is presented.

11. Enter records in the Data Form dialog box, pressing Tab between each field and Enter at the end of a record.

12. When you are finished entering records, click OK to go to the main document, or click View Source to go directly to the data table.

Editing Records and Managing Fields

When the active file is a data source file, Word automatically displays a Database toolbar:

From the toolbar, you can conveniently access tools you will use to manage the data source. You can enter new records, edit, or delete records in the data source just as you would in any table.

To add a new record to the end of your data source, click the Add New Record button on the Database toolbar, or press Tab in the last cell of the table.

 To delete a record, move the insertion point within the record you want to delete; then click the Delete Record button on the Database toolbar. Be careful not to delete the first row that contains the field names. If you do, you will have to recreate it to use this file as a data source.

WARNING After you chose the field names in the Create Data Source dialog box, you were prompted to save the data file. However, the file you saved was field names only—no data! Remember to resave the file often when you're entering data so that the records themselves are saved.

 To add, remove, or rename fields in your data source, click the Manage Fields button to open the Manage Fields dialog box:

 If you prefer to enter or view records using the data form, click the Data Form button on the toolbar to reopen the Data Form dialog box.

TIP You can convert an existing table to a data source by deleting text that precedes the table in the document, deleting any blank rows in the table itself, and renaming column headers so that they follow field name conventions. Word 2000 will recognize a document that meets these requirements as a data source. To use other database options with your table, choose View ➤ Toolbars to turn on the Database toolbar.

Editing Records and Managing Fields in Data Source View

1. Click the View Source button in the Data Form dialog box.

2. Click the Add New Record button to move to an empty row.

3. Click a record you want to delete and click the Delete Record button.

4. Make editing changes just as you would in any other table.

5. Choose Manage Fields to add, remove, or rename fields in the data source.

6. Click the Data Form button to reopen the Data Form dialog box.

Sorting It Out

Objective W2000E.5.3

You can organize your data source by sorting it on any field: last name, zip code, or any other field that you find useful. Records can be sorted in *ascending order* (A to Z, or 0 to 9) or in *descending order* (Z to A, or 9 to 0).

  To sort the records in the data source, place the insertion point anywhere in the column you want to sort by. Click the Sort Ascending or Sort Descending button on the Database toolbar to sort the records in the order you specified.

Sorting a Data Source

1. Open a data source document in Data Source view.

2. Move the insertion point to the column that you want to sort by.

3. Click the Sort Ascending or Sort Descending button on the Database toolbar.

Sorting Lists, Paragraphs, and Tables

Objective W2000E.1.3

You can sort any list in Word, whether or not it's a data source. You can sort regular tables, bulleted lists, and even ordinary paragraphs. First, select what you want to sort. Choose Table ➤ Sort from the menu bar to open the Sort dialog box.

If you've clicked a table or data source, the Sort By drop-down list shows you a list of field names based on the header row of the table. If you've selected a bulleted list or several paragraphs of text, the Sort By list only gives you two options: Paragraphs and Field 1. Choose Paragraphs to sort by the first word in each paragraph, or Field 1 to sort by the first field or tabular column. Choose whether the type of data you want to sort is text, numbers, or dates, and select ascending or descending order. If you are sorting data in a table or data source, you can indicate up to three sort levels. If your table has a header row, mark the Header Row button. When you have entered all the sort criteria, click OK to process the sort.

WARNING It's a good idea to save your document before you sort, and always check your data immediately after a sort to make sure it sorted correctly. If it did not, click Undo, or close the document without saving and reopen your saved copy.

Sorting Lists, Tables, and Paragraphs

1. Select the data you want to sort.

2. Choose Table ➤ Sort.

3. Enter what you want to sort by, the type of data you are sorting, and the sort order (ascending or descending).

4. If you're sorting a table, enter additional sort levels, if desired, and indicate if there is a header row.

5. Click OK to process the sort.

Hands On

Objectives E.5.2, E.5.3, and E.1.3

1. Create a data source file that contains information about your friends and family.

   a) Include fields that will give maximum flexibility in retrieving the data. The file should contain the following information: name, address, phone number, birth date, spouse/significant other's name, other.

   b) Enter at least 10 records. Leave fields blank if you do not have the information.

   c) Sort alphabetically by last name.

2. Open a document that contains a table.

   a) Convert the table to a data source. Resave the document under a different name.

   b) Switch to the Data Form dialog box (choose View ➤ Toolbars ➤ Database and click the Data Form button) and enter at least five new records.

   c) Sort the records alphabetically.

3. Open or create a document with a bulleted list and sort the list in descending order. Sort it again in ascending order.

Creating Customized Merge Documents

Whether you want to send a letter to 5 people or 500, you can use Word 2000 to personalize each one and create mailing labels or envelopes. You've heard about mail merge, and you may even have used it, but it's never been more foolproof than it is in Word 2000. And don't let the term *mail merge* limit your thinking: You can use mail merge to create telephone directories, birthday lists, nametags, you name it!

Creating a Main Merge Document

Objective W2000E.5.1

Before you can create a main document, you must have the data source in place. This can be a data source file you created in Word, an Excel list, an Access table or query, or a delimited text file you import from some other application. Create or identify your data source before proceeding with this section (review the previous section if you need help creating a data source).

After you've created a Word data source or identified a data source created in Excel, Access, or as a delimited text file in some other application, open the Mail Merge Helper (choose Tools ➤ Mail Merge) and click Create to create a main document. You have four choices of main documents.

Form Letters or reports you want to personalize

Mailing Labels or any other kind of label, such as nametags, video tape or disk labels, or file folder labels

Envelopes fed directly into your printer

Catalogs of data such as phone lists or membership directories—any data you want listed consecutively rather than on separate pages.

Word will ask if you want to use the current document or begin in a new document window. If the current window is empty, you can choose either option. If the current window contains a document into which you want to insert mail merge codes, choose Active Window. In all other cases, you should begin in a new window. Word again displays the Mail Merge Helper. Click the Get Data button and choose Open Data Source. In the Open Data Source dialog box, select the data source to use with the main document you are creating. After the data source is confirmed, Word will return to the main document and open a dialog box to remind you that the main document has no merge fields, so you cannot merge the main document and data source yet. Choose Edit Main Document to open the Mail Merge toolbar and begin creating the main document:

A main document contains two kinds of text: *regular text* and *variable text*. Regular text will be the same in each version of the merged document—like the body text within a letter. Variable text is represented by a *merge field*. Merge fields take the place of text that will be different in each merged document—for example, the recipient's name and address.

In the main document, enter, edit, and format regular text as you would in any Word document. Insert a merge field where you want text from the data source to appear in your final, merged document: Place the insertion point where you want the merge field to appear, then click the Insert Merge Field button on the Mail Merge toolbar to display the list of field names from the data source:

Choose the field name from the list, and Word inserts the merge field, as shown in Figure 4.4.

As soon as you've set up the main document the way you want it, you'll want to save it for use in future merges. When you use an existing main document, open the main document before you start the Mail Merge Helper. When you are prompted by the Helper to use the active document or to create a new main document, choose the active document.

TIP When you save a merge document, it's a good idea to indicate the type of document somewhere in the filename. We suggest you begin main documents with the word Main and when appropriate, the name of the data source it is linked to (Main-Acknowledgment Letter to Clients), so you can identify your main documents easily.

F I G U R E 4.4: Main document with merge codes

August 29, 1999

«Title» «FirstName» «LastName»
«JobTitle»
«Company»
«Address1»
«Address2»
«City», «State» «PostalCode»

Dear «Title» «LastName»:

We are excited about the prospect of working with you on the Web-based economic development program in your region. We believe that the use of an intranet to communicate with businesses in your communities is a critical part of your overall strategy and are looking forward to developing an attractive, easy-to-navigate Web site full of valuable information for all those involved. Int*net technology is moving so fast that every day there are new tools available to make your visions a reality. We will be submitting a proposal to you by the end of next week, and we can then meet to discuss the project in more detail.

Again, thanks for the opportunity , and we'll look forward to hearing from you.

Sincerely,

Annette Marquis   Gini Courter

Creating a Main Document

1. Identify the data source file you want to use with this main document. Create and save a new one if necessary.

2. Start a new document or open a document you wish to convert to a main merge document, then choose Tools ➤ Mail Merge from the menu bar.

3. Choose Create and then select the type of main document that you want to create.

4. Indicate whether you want to use the document in the active window or to create a new main document.

5. Choose Get Data under Data Source to open an existing data source file (the one you identified in Step 1 above).

6. Click Edit Main Document to enter the regular text in the main document.

Creating a Main Document *(continued)*

7. Move the insertion point to the position where you want data from the data source to appear. Click Insert Merge Field and select field names from the list to insert merge fields at the desired positions.

8. Save the main document.

Previewing the Merged Document

You've almost done it! When the main document and data source are merged, Word will generate a separate document or listing (if you are setting up a catalog) for each record in the data source based on the layout of the main document.

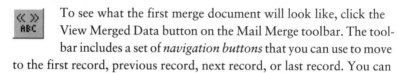 To see what the first merge document will look like, click the View Merged Data button on the Mail Merge toolbar. The toolbar includes a set of *navigation buttons* that you can use to move to the first record, previous record, next record, or last record. You can preview all the merged documents using the navigation buttons:

Click again on the View Merged Data button to return to the main document.

Merging Documents

Objective W2000E.5.4

You have created a main document and specified a data source. If everything looked OK when you previewed the merge results, you are ready for the actual merge. If the main document is not active, activate the main document window. The Mail Merge toolbar gives you a number of options, depending on how confident you are that everything is set the way you want it.

The most daring choice is Merge to Printer. Choose this option *only* if you have previewed your merge and everything is in perfect order. (Check that nobody has left purple and green paper in the printer!)

A much more conservative choice is Merge to New Document. Word will conduct the merge and create a new document with the results. This gives you the intermediate step of viewing the actual results of the merge before printing it. Once the merge is printed, there is no reason to save the merge results. If you need to print it again at a later date, you'll want to do the merge again, in case you've updated any of the records in the data source.

Your final option is to use the Merge dialog box, shown in Figure 4.5. Click the Merge button on the toolbar to open it.

F I G U R E 4.5: Merge dialog box

Here, you can choose to merge to a new document, a printer, an e-mail, or a fax, and you can specify only a portion of the records to merge. If you want Word to ignore blank fields (for instance, Address2 for records without a suite number), indicate that by checking the appropriate box.

Merging from an Alternate Data Source

Objective W2000E.5.6

If your data is kept in another application, an Excel Spreadsheet or an Outlook address book for example, you can easily merge it with a main document in Word. Open the Mail Merge Helper and proceed as you would with any merge. At the Get Data step, choose Open Data Source (if your data is in Excel, Access, or another database application) or choose Use Address Book to retrieve data from Outlook.

If you're attaching to an Excel or Access data source, you'll see the Open Data Source dialog box. Navigate to the drive and the folder that contains the data file, change the Files of Type drop-down to indicate the type of file you're looking for, select it, and then click Open. With an Excel data source, you will be prompted to choose whether to use the Entire Spreadsheet or a named range you've created in the worksheet. Proceed with creating the main document as you normally would.

TIP Excel is a powerful tool for managing non-relational databases. The *Microsoft Office User Certification Specialist Study Guide for Excel 2000*, also from Sybex,is an excellent resource to learn the application.

When you attach to an Outlook address book, you may be prompted to select a profile from a list. Once you complete this step, the Outlook fields are available to you from the Insert Merge Field drop-down list on the Mail Merge toolbar.

Specifying Records to Merge

Suppose you have a list of names and addresses and only want to send letters to people in a certain zip code or state. You can *filter* records based on criteria that you establish. After you select your data source and main document, click the Merge button to open the Merge dialog box. In the database world, a *query* is a tool used to select a group of records that meet specific criteria. Click the Query Options button to open the Filter Records page of the Query Options dialog box, shown in Figure 4.6.

F I G U R E 4.6: Query Options dialog box

In the Field drop-down list, select the field you want to use to select records. If, for example, you want to merge records with zip code 48439, choose the PostalCode field. To send letters to all the customers whose last name is Jones, choose LastName. In the Compare To control (at the far right of the dialog box), enter the text string you are looking for in the selected field: **48439** or **Jones**. The comparison box lets you determine how the records in the data source are compared to the text string.

Using And and Or

Once you enter a Compare To text string, the word *And* appears in the drop-down to the left of the second row of the Query Options dialog box. You can enter multiple query criteria and select, for example, the records for people in California where the data source doesn't list a zip code. The single most confusing thing about writing queries is knowing when to use And and when to use Or. If you can master this, you qualify as an expert query writer!

Choosing And means both comparisons must be true for a match. If you enter the Field, Comparison, and Compare To information in the example given above, choosing And will select all records where the State is California *and* the PostalCode field in the data source is blank. Records for people from Arkansas, Oregon, or Massachusetts will not be selected. Records for people living in California with a zip code will not be selected. Choosing Or means a match will be found if either comparison is true. In this case, *all* Californians will be selected, as well as anyone from any other state who doesn't have a zip code listed in the data source.

Use Or when you want to select two possible values for the same field. If you select records where State is equal to California *and* State is equal to Nevada, no records will be selected (since no single record includes both states). Choosing Or will select records for both states.

Use And when you want to select records from a numeric range. For example, you might want to send an advertisement to all families with annual incomes between $25,000 and $40,000. In this example, you select Income Greater Than 25000 And Income Less Than 40000. If you used Or, all records would be selected, as every level of income is either less than 40000 or more than 25000.

TIP   Here's a general rule for troubleshooting queries: If you expected some records to be selected but none were, you probably used And when you should have used Or. If you got a lot more records than you expected, you probably used Or when you should have used And.

Sorting Records

Objective W2000E.5.3

After you select your merge criteria, you can also choose how you want your data sorted by clicking the Sort Records tab on the Query Options dialog box. Use the skills you learned in the previous section to set the sort criteria. When you've finished setting your query options, click OK, and you're ready to merge.

Selecting and Sorting Records to Merge

1. Choose the Merge button from the Mail Merge toolbar.

2. Click Query Options to open the Query Options dialog box.

3. Select the field you want to use to select (filter) records.

4. Choose a comparison criterion.

5. Enter the text string you are looking for in the Compare To control.

6. Enter other desired query criteria by selecting And or Or and then selecting the criteria.

7. Click the Sort Records tab to sort the resulting merged document.

8. Select the desired sort fields and indicate whether you want the records to be sorted in ascending or descending order.

9. Choose OK to return to the Merge dialog box.

10. Preview the merge, if you wish, by clicking the View Merged Data button on the Mail Merge toolbar. Click Merge to begin the merge.

Creating Catalogs and Lists

A *catalog* main document is used to create lists; each record is listed directly under the previous record on the same page. You might use the Catalog option to create, for instance, an employee phone directory. Word doesn't shine its brightest with catalogs. However, if you know how to work around the awkwardness of Word's catalog merge, it's still the most convenient way to present a list of the records in a data source.

When you choose Catalog as the main document type from the Mail Merge Helper, in the main document, you can either create a table to hold the merge field codes or use tabs to separate the codes. We encourage you to use a table; it produces consistent results with the least amount of hassle. Enter any text you want to appear with each *record* of the data source, but don't include other surrounding text. If, for example, you want a heading to appear above the records in the list, *don't* enter it now or your merged document will include a heading, a record, another heading, another record, and so forth.

You can click the View Merged Data button to see each individual record as it will appear in the merged document, but you have to actually do the merge to see them all together. You can sort or select records before merging using Query Options.

After you merge the data source and main document, you can add titles, column headings, and any other information to the merged document before you print it. Merged catalogs are the exception to the suggestion that you not save merge results. If you have to add a lot of heading and title information after the merge, you may want to save it for future reference.

Using the Catalog Merge Feature

1. Choose Tools ➤ Mail Merge.

2. Create or open a main document and a data source. Select Catalog as the main document type.

Using the Catalog Merge Feature *(continued)*

3. Edit the main document to include any text you want to appear with each record and insert the field codes in the desired positions. Generally, you'll want this information in a table; however, you should not insert column headings at this point.

4. Preview the merge, using View Merged Data to see individual records in the merge.

5. Run the merge, setting query options to select and sort records as desired. Once you run the merge, you should see all records.

6. Add any additional text, headings, or titles to complete the document before printing.

7. Save the merge results document.

Creating Envelopes and Labels

Objective W2000E.5.5

Labels and envelopes are two other types of main documents. Word can merge to various sizes of envelopes: standard, business, note card, and other sizes. If your printer can print on envelopes and labels, you can create them in Word. (You must also know how to load the envelopes and labels. If you're not sure, consult your printer manual.)

To create labels, open the Mail Merge Helper and choose Mailing Labels from the Create Main Document drop-down list. After you select a data source, a dialog box will appear. Click the Set Up Main Document button. The Label Options dialog box opens (see Figure 4.7), offering you a choice of label sizes. You can select Avery, Formtec, Maco, and a host of other labels by choosing a brand from the Label Products list and scrolling through the list below it to select the number printed on the box. You may have to set the dimensions for other brands of labels not included on the Label Products list, but many other brands have the corresponding Avery number printed somewhere on the box.

F I G U R E 4.7: Label Options dialog box

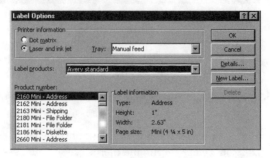

After you select a label, click the OK button to open the Create Labels dialog box (Figure 4.8).

F I G U R E 4.8: Create Labels dialog box

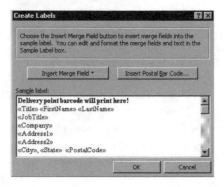

The Sample Label pane is like the main document window. Click the Insert Merge Field button to insert merge field codes in the label. Enter any other text from the keyboard. If you want to print a delivery point bar code to help out the post office, click Insert Postal Bar Code and identify which field holds the zip code and which is your main address field.

You won't find buttons to format in this dialog box, but you can right-click selected text and use the formatting options on the shortcut menu. Click OK to close the Create Labels dialog box and return to the Mail Merge Helper. Close the Mail Merge Helper and preview your labels before printing them. If you can't see all the needed text, it's easier to re-create the labels from scratch rather than editing them.

If you want to save the label document, you can close the Mail Merge Helper and save the main document, or you can wait until after you have merged the labels. Include the word *Labels* (instead of *Main*) at the beginning of the filename.

Creating Envelopes

Follow the same initial steps for envelopes that you did when you were creating labels. When you click the Create button in the Mail Merge Helper, choose Envelopes rather than Mailing Labels. Select the Envelope Size from the list provided. (You even have options for how to format your envelope; click one of the Font buttons to see them.) Choose OK to proceed to the Envelope Address dialog box. Insert merge field names just as you did in the Create Labels dialog box. When you close the Envelope Address dialog box, Word will return you to the Mail Merge Helper so you can merge envelopes.

Creating Labels Using Mail Merge

1. Choose Tools ➤ Mail Merge.

2. Click Create and choose Mailing Labels as the document type.

3. Click Get Data and choose a data source. Click Set Up Main Document to open the Label Options dialog box.

4. Select a label brand from the Label Products list, then scroll down the list of label options and select the label type that you want to use. Click OK.

5. Enter field codes as desired.

6. Select the field codes you have entered and right-click to change the formatting of the text.

7. Click Insert Postal Bar Code to create a bar code on each label.

8. Click OK when you are finished setting up the label to see the main document.

9. Preview the labels to make sure all the lines print on each label.

Troubleshooting Merge Problems

There are three basic reasons for merge problems:

- Document incompatibility
- Problems with the data source
- Problems with the main document.

Document incompatibility means that either the data source or the main document isn't a valid Word mail merge file. A dialog box will appear telling you that the main document has no merge codes or that the data source is invalid. Examine the file in question. If it is a data file, make sure it has field names, that there is no extra text at the beginning of the file, and that the data is in a table or is properly delimited. If the problem is the main document, open it and check to make sure you have selected the correct file and that it has merge field codes. (Remember, you must enter merge field codes from the toolbar; you cannot type << before the field name and >> after.) Even if both files seem to be OK, structural problems with individual records (such as missing fields) can cause Word to stop in the middle of a merge.

 You can have Word check the data source for omission errors before merging. With the main document active, click the Check for Errors button on the Mail Merge toolbar to open the Checking and Reporting Errors dialog box, shown in Figure 4.9. This is much like checking spelling before printing.

F I G U R E 4.9: Checking for data source errors

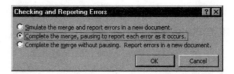

You can choose to have Word simulate a merge or actually merge the two documents and report errors. If you expect errors, simulation is best. If you don't think there will be errors (always our hope), go ahead and have Word merge; it stops along the way to report any errors it finds. When Word finds an error, a dialog box opens. Depending on the kind of error, you may be allowed to fix the error and then continue merging. If you cannot, note the information provided, and click the OK button to continue finding errors. When Error Checking is complete, close the merged document and fix the data source and/or main document files before merging the documents again.

Even if Word finds no errors and your documents merge, you may still find mistakes in your merged document. There is an easy way to decide if a mistake is in the main document or in the data source:

- If the mistake appears in every merged document, look for the problem in the main document. For example, if there is no space between the first and last names in your merged form letters, you should put a space between the merge codes for FirstName and LastName in the main document. Spelling errors in every merged document should lead you to suspect that you forgot to check the spelling in the main document before merging.

- If a mistake appears in some, but not all, merged documents, the problem is in the data source. If a merged first name is spelled incorrectly in one of the merged letters, it's misspelled in the data source. Close the merged file, open the data source file, and correct the error. Then merge the documents again.

Hands On

Objectives W2000E.5.1, E.5.4, E.5.5, and E.5.6

1. Create a form letter with field codes to represent data in an existing data source file.

   a) Preview the merge to see that everything is correct.

   b) Merge to a new document.

   c) Be sure to save your data source file (if you made any changes to it) and your main document. Discard the merge document without saving changes.

2. Create mailing labels to a select group of people from an existing data source file.

    a) Select only those people on the list who meet certain criteria (from the same zip code, from the same city, name begins with the same letter, and so on).

    b) Sort the records to merge by Last Name.

3. Create a catalog main document using an alternate data source (an Excel spreadsheet or an Outlook address book, for example).

    a) Use a table to hold your fields.

    b) Merge the main document with the data source.

    c) Add a title to the document and header rows to the columns.

    d) Format the table to improve its appearance.

    e) Print the table.

Publishing Online Forms

As more people have computers on their desktops and more computers are networked together, the paperless office is becoming a reality. One way that's happening is through the creation and use of online forms. If you need to create a vacation request form, why go to the trouble of creating the form, printing it, making copies, and distributing them? With an online form, an employee opens the form online, fills it out, and sends it by e-mail to the supervisor, who approves (or disapproves) it and returns the e-mail. It's all over in a matter of minutes—no copies, no lost forms, no missed vacations.

Designing a Form

Objective W2000E.6.4

Because you'll want to use the online form over and over again, you need to create your form as a template. Choose File ➢ New, choose Blank Document from the General tab, click Template from the Create New options at the bottom right of the dialog box, and then click OK:

The new template will open as Template1. It's not a bad idea to save it now so you can quickly save changes as you create the form. Since you've identified this as a template, the Save As dialog box opens to the Templates folder and shows the file type as Document Template.

 Save the template in one of the existing template folders, or create a new folder for online forms. Creating a new folder in the Templates folder causes it to be displayed as a Tab in the New dialog box. Once you save the new template, it will be available for users to select when they create a new document.

Before you start creating your form, sketch it on paper or use an existing hard-copy form as a model. This gives your online form a better ultimate design and saves you the time and frustration of trying to design the form while you're creating it. Once you have decided on a design, right-click any toolbar and activate the Forms toolbar:

The Forms toolbar includes buttons to insert form fields, to create tables and frames to position questions and prompts on the page, to turn form-field shading on or off, and to protect the form so that users can only enter data where you have placed fields.

The easiest way to lay out the form is by using a table. Tables allow you to place text on different parts of the screen without worrying about user-entered text wrapping to a new line.

Click the Draw Table or Insert Table button on the Forms toolbar to create a table. (Feel free to review the Tables section in Chapter 3 if you need a refresher on using these tools.) Figure 4.10 shows an example of an online form that was created using tables. The gridlines and borders have been turned off except for the bottom borders, which form the lines for users' responses.

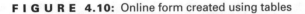

F I G U R E 4.10: Online form created using tables

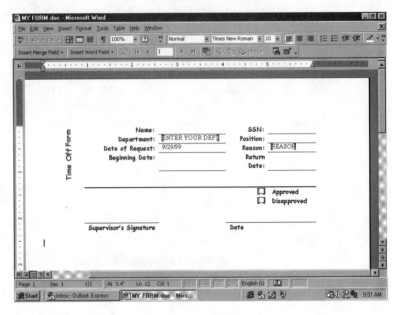

Figure 4.11 shows the same form with table gridlines turned on. As you can see, rows and columns aren't evenly distributed, and extra cells have been inserted to provide the appropriate spacing for items on the form.

After you enter field names and prompts in the table, you can split cells, merge cells, change borders, and adjust column and row widths as needed. Since the form is to be viewed online, don't forget to add colors, shading, and graphics to really make an impression. For more information about working with graphics, see Chapter 5. See "Adding Field Controls" in this chapter for more detail on adding fields.

F I G U R E 4.11: Online form showing gridlines

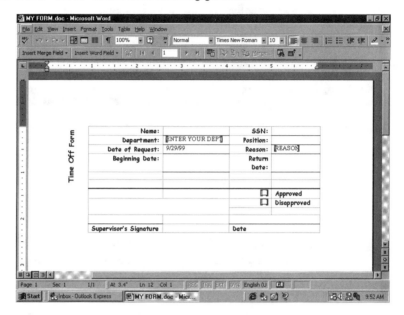

Using Frames and Text Boxes

The Forms toolbar has an option for frames, which allow you to place an item precisely at any position on a form. You may want to frame small tables so you can position them easily on the page.

Click the Insert Frame button, drag a rectangle the approximate size of your table, and then insert a table into the frame. You can resize a frame by pointing to one of the black handles around its borders. When the mouse pointer changes to a double-headed arrow, you can drag the handle. To reposition the frame, click the frame to select it, and with the four-headed arrow mouse pointer, drag the frame to a new position.

TIP Insert frames after you've entered and edited the appropriate fields in the table you're framing.

If it's text you want to position, however, Word's text box feature, found on the Drawing toolbar, is a much more flexible option. With text boxes, you can apply 3-D effects, shadows, fills, and backgrounds, and in addition to changing the orientation of the text, you can flip and rotate the boxes themselves. For more information about text boxes, see Chapter 5.

Designing a Form

1. Open the New dialog box, choose Blank Document, and click Template in the Create New option. Click OK to create a blank template.

2. Choose File ➢ Save As to save the template in the most appropriate template folder. Give the template a descriptive name.

3. Display the Forms toolbar by right-clicking any toolbar and choosing Forms from the list.

4. Design the form using a table for the body of the form. Add bottom borders where appropriate to provide user-response lines.

5. Save the template.

Adding Field Controls

Objective W2000E.6.1 and E.6.5

Once your form is laid out, you must add *fields* or placeholders that other people can use to submit their information. You can access three types of fields from buttons on the Forms toolbar.

 Text fields—These are open fields of any length where users can enter text.

 Check Box fields—Users can check or clear these boxes to indicate answers.

 Drop-Down fields—Users choose a response from a list of choices you provide.

When your form is completed and you turn on protection, users will only be able to enter text or choices in the fields. The rest of the document will be off-limits to them.

To insert a field, position your cursor where you would like the field to appear, and then click one of the three form field buttons found on the left end of the toolbar, either Text, Check Box, or Drop-Down.

 It's helpful to have the Form Field Shading button turned on while you are creating the form so that you can see where the fields are.

After you enter a field, specify the options you want to apply to the field. Double-click the field to open the appropriate Form Field Options dialog box. The options for text form fields, shown in Figure 4.12, include:

Type—Regular text, number, date, current date, current time, or calculation.

Default Text—If there is a response that users would most commonly give, making it the default means they will only have to enter responses that differ from the default.

Maximum Length—Unlimited or a specified number of characters, which limits the length of user entries.

Text Format—Uppercase, Lowercase, First Capital, or Title Case to format user entries.

F I G U R E 4.12: Text Form Field Options dialog box

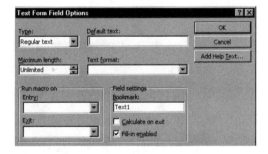

You can also run macros on entry into and exit from a field (see Chapter 7 for more information about macros), set bookmarks, or have Word calculate the field on exit. If you want to restrict user access to a field, you can clear the Fill-in Enabled check box.

The Add Help Text option will endear you forever to your users:

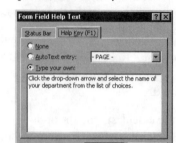

Use this option to add text to the status bar and provide even more detailed instructions when users press the F1 key. Just click Type Your Own and enter whatever text you would like to have appear when the user moves into the field.

The unique options for check box form fields, shown in Figure 4.13, include:

Check Box Size—Choose either Auto (makes your check box the size of the text), or Exactly (lets you designate how large the box will be).

Default Value—Determines whether or not the box is checked when the form opens.

F I G U R E 4.13: Check Box Form Field Options dialog box

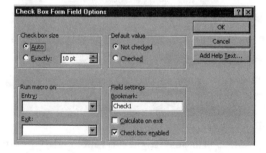

The only unique option for drop-down form fields, shown in Figure 4.14, is the list of drop-down items, which you must supply. Enter the text in the Drop-Down Item text box and click the Add button. After you create your list, you can use the Move buttons to rearrange the items. Select an

item and click Remove to delete or edit an item from the list. Unfortunately, the first item always shows up on the form as if it is the default. The only way around this is to enter a blank item (press the spacebar a few times before you click Add), or to make the first item instructional: Select your department. However, if you provide either of these options, you cannot prevent users from selecting these as their choice, so think carefully about this before deciding which way you want to go.

F I G U R E 4.14: Drop-Down Form Field Options dialog box

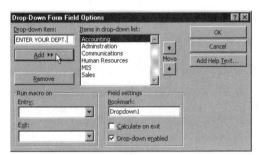

When your form is ready to distribute, you may want to turn off Form Field Shading (click the Form Field Shading button). This is purely optional, but because the shading does not correspond to the actual length of the field, it can give users the wrong impression about how much they should enter in a field.

Adding Form Fields

1. Click the space where you want the field to appear. Click the Text Form Field, Check Box Form Field, or Drop-Down Form Field button on the Forms toolbar to insert the field.

2. Double-click the field to edit the form field options.

3. Enter text, check box, and drop-down list options, as appropriate.

4. Click the Add Help Text button to insert your own status bar and F1 Help key instructions into the form.

5. Click OK to save the help instructions and OK again to return to your form.

6. When you are finished setting options in all the fields, you can click the Form Field Shading button to hide the shading, if desired.

Protecting and Using the Form

Your form is almost ready to distribute. One more step will make sure that your template stays intact and that users have access only to the field controls.

 After you're sure everything is exactly the way you want it, click the Protect Form button on the Forms toolbar. When you do this, you will no longer have access to most toolbar and menu options. However, you can still save your template, and that's exactly what you want to do next.

When users open a protected form, they will only be able to click the field controls. Pressing Tab and Shift+Tab will move forward and backward through the fields. They will have limited access to toolbars and other options. They can enter their information, send it to the printer, and name and save the document.

After protecting your form, it's always smart to test the form by filling it out to check that the tab order is correct. *Tab order* is the order in which the fields are activated when you press Tab. Depending on how you created the table and positioned the items in it, it may not tab logically through the fields. To correct this, you may have to insert blank cells or reposition items on the form. You may also find that you made a field's length too short or that you didn't include all the options in a drop-down list. Use the form as if you were one of your potential users; if possible, ask a colleague to test the form for you. It's amazing how easy it is to overlook something when you already know what data is expected in a field.

If you need to edit the form, be sure to open the template and not just a copy of the form. To open the template, choose File ➤ Open, change the Files of Type control to Document Templates (*.dot), locate the form in the appropriate template folder (the default folder is `C:\Program Files\Microsoft Office\Templates`), and click Open. You can then turn on the Forms toolbar and click the Protect Form button. You will again have free rein to do whatever you want to the form (within reason, of course!).

Protecting and Testing the Form

1. Click the Protect Form button on the Forms toolbar to restrict user access to just the field controls on the form. Resave the form.

2. Open the form as a user would by clicking File ➤ New and choosing it from the dialog box. Test the tab order by pressing Tab through the form and making sure it proceeds in a logical order.

3. Enter data in each field and see what happens if a user enters incorrect data (too much or too little, for example).

4. To edit the form, choose File ➤ Open, change Files of Type to Document Template (*.dot), select the template from the template folders, and click Open.

5. Turn on the Forms toolbar (choose View ➤ Toolbars ➤ Forms) and click the Protect Form button to turn protection off.

6. Correct any tab-order problems by rearranging fields or inserting blank cells in the table.

7. Make additional editing changes as desired, click Protect Form again, and save the template.

Using an Online Form

1. Choose File ➤ New and choose the form from the New dialog box.

2. Press Tab to navigate forward and Shift+Tab to navigate backward through the fields.

3. Save or print the new document as desired.

Hands On

Objectives W2000E.6.1, E.6.4, and E.6.5

1. Design a form similar to the one shown in Figure 4.11. It can be the same form or one of your own design.

   a) Create a new blank template to hold your form.

b) Enter and format the form title and other information.

c) Create a table to hold the body of your form. Use each type of field control where appropriate. Set the options for each control, including length for text fields.

d) Set the Text format of one of the text fields for Title Case.

e) Protect, save, and close the form when you have finished designing it.

2. Open the form as if you were a user (choose File ➤ New) and enter data in each field. Note any problems with the form. Close the form without saving changes.

3. Reopen the template and turn off form protection. Make any needed editing changes identified when you tested the form. Turn on protection, save, and retest the form.

Adding References to Your Documents

Adding footnotes, endnotes, tables of contents, indexes, and cross-references makes your documents easy to follow and helps your readers find what they are looking for. When you plan ahead, Word 2000 takes the headache out of these additional touches, providing one more way for your work to stand out.

Adding Footnotes and Endnotes

Objective W2000E.2.8

When you want to provide readers with more information about your topic, Word 2000 gives you options for inserting both *footnotes*, which appear at the bottom of the page, and *endnotes*, which appear at the end of the document. Word automatically numbers the notes for you and calculates how much space footnotes will need at the bottom of the page. Where was this feature when we were typing term papers?

To insert a footnote or an endnote, position the insertion point where you'd like the *reference mark* (footnote or endnote number) to appear and choose Insert ➤ Footnote. The Footnote and Endnote dialog box opens. Select the type of note you want to insert.

You can choose traditional automatic numbering (1, 2, 3) or insert a custom mark or symbol. After you make your numbering selection, Word inserts the reference mark and, depending on the current view, either opens a note pane (Normal view) or takes you to the actual location where the note will appear in your document (Print Layout view).

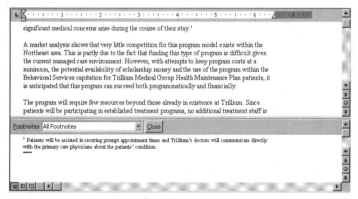

It's much easier to work with notes in Normal view because you can enter your note in the pane and click Close when you are finished. In Print Layout view, you must find your way back to where you inserted the reference mark. In either view, when you want to review your note, all you have to do is point to the reference mark.

The mouse pointer will change to a note, and a moment later, the note will appear.

The Trillium Extended Stay Treatment (TEST) is an innovative, cost-effective program designed to provide the additional support that patients need when transitioning from residential treatment to outpatient services. Today, all patients are discharged from residential treatment to return home as they begin participation in day-treatment or intensi~ Patients will be assisted in securing the Extended Stay Treatment will continue to live at Trilliun prompt appointment times and Trillium's treatment. The primary difference between these patients an doctors will communicate directly with the residential program will be the amount of medical care that { primary care physicians about the responsible for seeing their primary care physicians in the ar patients' condition. significant medical concerns arise during the course of their stay.

Just move the mouse pointer away and the note disappears.

Creating Footnotes and Endnotes

1. Switch to Normal view. Place the insertion point where you want the reference mark to appear.

2. Choose Insert ➤ Footnote.

3. Indicate whether you want automatic numbering or a custom mark. You can type in a custom mark or choose one from the Symbol font sets.

4. Enter your note in the Footnotes or Endnotes box that opens at the bottom of the screen. Click Close when you are finished entering your note.

5. To view the note, point to the reference mark in your document. The note will appear as a yellow ScreenTip.

Revising Footnotes and Endnotes

Now that you have footnotes and endnotes scattered through your text, you may need to edit one of the notes. Just double-click any reference mark in Normal view to open the Footnotes or Endnotes window at the bottom of the screen. All notes of the same type appear in the same window—just scroll to the one you want to edit, make your changes, and click Close.

Deleting Notes

When you want to delete a note entirely, click before or after the reference mark and press the Backspace or Delete key twice—the first time will select the reference mark and the second time will delete both the mark and the note. Subsequent footnotes will automatically be renumbered.

Deleting the text inside the note pane or at the bottom or end of the document will not delete the reference mark.

Revising and Deleting Notes

1. To revise a note, double-click any reference mark to open the note pane (in Normal view). Make changes and click Close.

2. To delete a note, select and delete the reference mark in the body of the document.

Using Bookmarks

Objective W2000E.2.3

It's useful to be able to mark a location in the text that you want to return to later, especially when you are working with long documents. This could be a place where you need to insert some additional information before finishing the final draft. Or if your document will be read online, the location could refer to a piece of text you want readers to be able to jump to quickly. Whatever the reason, by inserting bookmarks you can easily move to specific text or objects in a document without having to scroll.

To insert a bookmark, select the text, graphic, table, or other object you want to mark. Choose Insert ➤ Bookmark. The Bookmark dialog box opens so you can name the bookmark. Names must be one word but you can use upper- and lowercase:

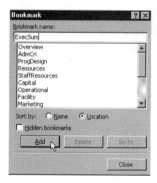

Click Add to add the bookmark and close the dialog box. (You can also delete bookmarks here by selecting the bookmark and clicking Delete.) To find bookmarks easily in the dialog box, sort them alphabetically or by their relative location in the document.

To see the bookmarks in your text, you can either go back to the Bookmark dialog box or choose Tools ➤ Options and click Show Bookmarks on the View page. The bookmarks will be displayed in brackets:

⟦EXECUTIVE SUMMARY⟧

The brackets are nonprinting characters, so if you're working a lot with bookmarks, it's handy just to leave them turned on.

When you want to go to a bookmark, choose Go To from the Browse Object menu at the bottom of the vertical scroll bar. Select Bookmarks from the Go To What list, and then click the drop-down arrow next to the Enter Bookmark Name text box to see a list of the bookmarks in your document:

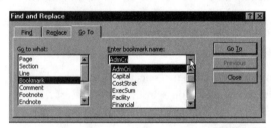

Select the bookmark you want to go to, click Go To and *voilà*, you are there. The Go To dialog box stays open until you close it, so to move to another bookmark, choose it from the list, and click Go To again.

 When you close the Go To dialog box, you can use the Browse buttons to move through all your bookmarks.

Inserting, Viewing, and Deleting Bookmarks

1. Select the item you want to bookmark.

2. Choose Insert ➤ Bookmark and either accept the entire selected name or enter another name (names must be one word). Click Add.

3. View all the bookmarks in a document by choosing Tools ➤ Options ➤ View and clicking Show Bookmarks.

4. To jump to a bookmark, open the Browse Object menu, choose Go To, select Bookmark, and choose the bookmark from the Enter Bookmark Name drop-down list. Click Go To.

5. To delete a bookmark, select the bookmark and click Delete.

Creating Cross-References

Objectives W2000.4.8 and E.2.11

There are two reasons to use cross-references: to *refer to* text or objects elsewhere in a document, or to allow users to *move to* referenced text or objects. The traditional cross-reference is the first type and is used to keep references within a document up to date throughout editing. In the text, you might direct a reader to see a paragraph in Chapter 5: See Employee Benefits for more information. If the Employee Benefits section is later moved to Chapter 4, you can rest assured that they will still look in the right place, because the cross-reference will be updated when the Employee Benefits section is moved.

The second kind of cross-reference is a hyperlink, commonly used in Internet sites. A *hyperlink* is a connection between two areas of a document or two different documents; users move directly to the Employee Benefits section by clicking the hyperlink. On the Web, hyperlinks are underlined and use a different font color (if they don't stand out, no one knows to click them!). You'll have to format your hyperlinks' font colors and apply underlining. The cross-referencing feature does not do it automatically.

To insert a cross-reference, position your insertion point where you want the reference to appear and type your introductory text. (`"For more information on Digital Mastering, see"`). Choose Insert ➤ Cross-Reference to open the Cross-Reference dialog box and identify the text being referred to:

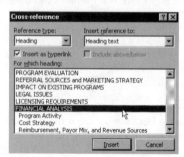

Cross-references can be linked to bookmarks, headings, numbered items, footnotes, endnotes, equations, figures, and tables—and you can choose how the reference will appear in the document. For example, if you want to refer to a heading, you can have the cross-reference indicate the actual text of the heading, the page number where the text is found, or just `see above` or `see below`.

If your document is intended for use online or on-screen, leave the Insert As Hyperlink check box checked. This creates the second, more active kind of cross-reference. When a user points to a hyperlinked cross-reference, the mouse pointer changes to a hand shape, and a ScreenTip appears telling the user where they will go if they click the hyperlink.

 Clicking once whisks the user off to the new location and automatically opens the Web toolbar so they can click the Back button to return to their point of origin.

TIP Do *not* use Insert As Hyperlink if you want a traditional, passive reference. If you do, every time you click near the cross-reference to edit surrounding text, you'll end up at the referenced text: an incredibly frustrating experience.

Creating Cross-References

1. Type the text to notify the reader of the cross-reference (See...).

2. Choose Insert ➤ Cross-Reference to open the Cross-Reference dialog box.

3. Select the Reference Type: for example, Bookmark.

4. Choose what the reference will refer to (page number, text, numbered item, and so on).

5. Identify the specific reference from the For Which list.

6. If you want the cross-reference to work as a hyperlink, make sure the Insert As Hyperlink box is checked.

7. Click Insert and type a close quote (") after the field that was inserted.

Be careful to not delete an item that is referenced or the link will be broken. If the cross-reference is a hyperlink, Word will take your readers to another location that contains similar text. Users clicking the See Employee Benefits hyperlink could find themselves, for example, on the Termination of Employment page—probably not the message you want to convey.

Indexing for Easy Reference

Objective W2000E.2.12

You can make lengthy documents more user-friendly by creating an index of key words and phrases. Although marking index text is a manual process, Word 2000 automates the creation of the index and will update it on request. When you're ready to mark your first entry, select the text you want to include in the index and press Alt+Shift+X to open the Mark Index Entry dialog box:

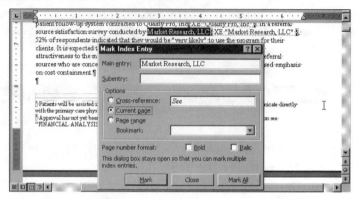

You can accept the selected text as the index entry or edit it any way you prefer. You can also add two subentries. Type the first subentry in the Subentry box, type a colon, and enter the second subentry. Click Mark to mark this specific selection, or Mark All to mark every occurrence of the text string for indexing. The Mark Index Entry dialog box will stay open while you return to your document and select the next text you want to appear in the index. When you click back in the dialog box, the selected text will appear in the Mark Index Entry text box.

If you want this entry to refer to another entry, click Cross-Reference and after the word *See,* type the name of the other entry, or type the word *also* and the name of the other entry. Because the cross-reference will only occur once in the index, you can Mark but not Mark All cross-references. To include a range of pages in the Index (such as `Formatting Text, 13-17`), you must first select the range and give it a bookmark name. You can then choose Page Range in the Mark Index Entry dialog box and select the name of the bookmark.

Close the Mark Index Entry dialog box when you're through, then move to the last page of your document. Insert a hard page break, then enter a heading for the index. Use a heading style if you want the index heading included in your table of contents later. Press Enter a couple of times to leave some space after the heading, and choose Insert ➤ Index and Tables. The

Index and Tables dialog box will open and you can choose how you'd like your index formatted, previewing your choices in the Print Preview pane.

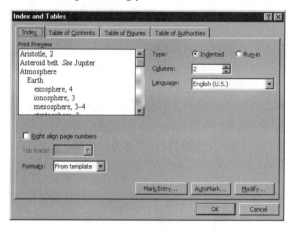

When you've made all your formatting choices, click OK. Your index will be generated automatically at the insertion point.

It's a good idea to go through each entry in the index and make sure it says what you want it to say and that the references are accurate. If you find any errors, you can fix them in the index or in the Index Entry (XE) fields inserted in the document, but any changes made to the index itself will be lost if you regenerate the index. After you make your changes to the XE fields, choose Insert ➤ Index and Tables again to regenerate the index. Word will select the existing index and ask you if you want to replace it.

Creating an Index

1. Select the first text you want to include in the index.

2. Press Alt+Shift+X to open the Mark Index Entry dialog box.

3. Type or edit the text in the Main Entry box.

4. Enter subentries in the Subentry box, placing a colon between second- and third-level entries.

5. Choose Mark or Mark All to mark all occurrences of the text in the document.

Creating an Index *(continued)*

6. To make additional entries, select the text and click the Mark Index Entry dialog box.

7. To include a cross-reference, choose Cross-Reference in the dialog box and type in the cross-reference text (See [name of entry]); choose Mark.

8. To include a range of pages, create a bookmark from the beginning to the end of the range, choose Range of Pages in the Mark Index Entry dialog box, and select the name of the bookmark you created.

9. To generate the index, move to a blank page, insert and format any heading text you want, choose Insert ➤ Index and Tables, and choose the desired formatting options. Click OK to create the index.

10. To regenerate the index, choose Insert ➤ Index and Tables and click OK again or click the index and press the F9 key.

Generating a Table of Contents

Objective W2000E.2.10

After creating an index, a table of contents (TOC) is a breeze: that is, of course, if you used heading styles when you created your document. If you didn't, the breeze just turned into gale-force winds—you need to go back through your document and apply styles to any text you want included in your table of contents.

To create the table of contents, move to the beginning of your document and insert a page break. Move to the blank page and choose Insert ➤ Index and Tables. Click the Table of Contents tab and choose from a number of built-in formats for your TOC.

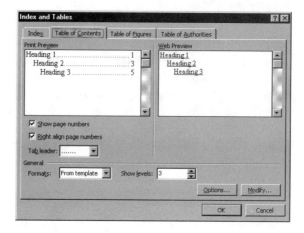

Choose a format and click OK. Add a heading, and your TOC should look something like the one in Figure 4.15.

F I G U R E 4.15: Table of Contents

Table of Contents

Modifying a TOC

You can edit directly in the TOC itself. When you click the TOC, it looks like the whole thing is selected, but you can still select text within it and make changes. If you decide that you want fewer heading levels to appear in your TOC, choose Insert ➤ Index and Tables ➤ Table of Contents and decrease the number of heading levels. You can also change the tab leader by selecting a different one from the Tab Leader list. When you click OK, the TOC will regenerate with the requested number of levels. In some documents, you may even want two TOCs—one with all heading levels and one with only the first-level headings.

Creating a Table of Contents

1. Apply heading styles to all the headings you want included in the TOC.

2. Create and move to a blank page at the beginning of the document.

3. Choose Insert ➤ Index and Tables. Click the Table of Contents tab.

4. Choose the format you want for your TOC, the number of heading levels, and the tab leader.

5. Click OK to generate the TOC.

6. Click the TOC and edit or reformat it directly or make changes to the headings in your document; regenerate the TOC by repeating steps 3–5, or by clicking it and pressing F9.

Hands On

Objectives W2000E.2.3, E.2.8, E.2.10, E.2.11, and E.2.12

1. Open an existing document or create a new document that has at least three headings and related paragraphs (be sure to apply styles to the headings):

    a) Switch to Normal view and add at least two footnotes and two endnotes to the document.

    b) Switch to Print Layout view and view the footnotes and endnotes at the bottom of the page.

    c) Point to one of the footnotes and read the note in the ScreenTip above the footnote marker.

    d) Delete the first footnote and the first endnote.

2. Using the same document you used in the first exercise:

    a) Create a bookmark to the first paragraph.

    b) Create a cross-reference to that bookmark from some later text.

    c) Create a second cross-reference to the second heading.

    d) Test both cross-references.

    e) Use Go To to move to the bookmark you created.

3. Using the same document:

    a) Go through the document and mark index entries for key terms, names, and other important words.

    b) Move to the end of the document, insert a page break, and generate the index.

4. Again in the same document:

    a) Move to the top of the document and insert a blank page for a table of contents.

    b) Generate the table of contents.

    c) Makes changes to one or more of your headings and regenerate the TOC.

Working Together on Documents

If you work in a networked office where people collaborate on written projects, Word 2000 offers a number of useful workgroup features. You can track document changes, save multiple versions within a document, and even edit a document simultaneously with your colleagues. This amazing group of features could actually put an end to interoffice squabbling over which *is* the latest version and who had it last.

Creating Master Documents

Objective W2000E.2.9

As a policy manual, personnel handbook, or similar document gets longer, it uses more resources to open, save, or print. It takes forever to scroll down a couple of pages and editing becomes a nightmare. With a little foresight, you can avoid this dilemma by starting with an outline and then dividing the document into various subdocuments. You and others in your work-group can then work with subdocuments as autonomous entities. How-ever, at any point, you can work with the entire master document, so you can have continuous page numbering, add headers and footers, create a table of contents, attach an index, and insert cross-references—all the stuff that contributes to another kind of nightmare if you try to do it with unre-lated documents.

What if you're already 10 chapters into an unruly document? Word 2000 can combine separate documents into one *master document* and divide one long document into several *subdocuments*. So there's no excuse for working with a document that's out of control—the remedy is right at your fingertips.

Creating a New Master Document

To create a new master document from scratch, open a new document, and then click the Outline View button. Word displays the Master Doc-ument toolbar to the right of the Outlining toolbar. Create an outline just as you normally would (see Chapter 3) using the same heading level for each section you want subdivided into its own document.

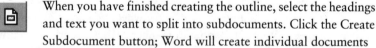 When you have finished creating the outline, select the headings and text you want to split into subdocuments. Click the Create Subdocument button; Word will create individual documents using the first part of the heading text for the document name. The master document will show the subdocuments in a distinct box with a small doc-ument icon in the upper-left corner.

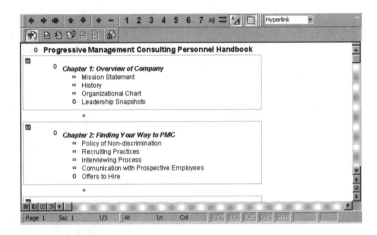

You can double-click any of the document icons to open a subdocument. Any changes you make in the subdocument are reflected in the master document when you save the subdocument.

 The primary purpose of creating a master document is to be able to work with discrete sections of the document. It makes sense, then, to collapse the master document so that just the document names are visible. Clicking the Collapse Subdocuments button on the Master Document toolbar will collapse the document, as shown in Figure 4.16. If you want to see all the text in the entire document, click the same button again (it's now the Expand Subdocuments button).

F I G U R E 4.16: A collapsed master document

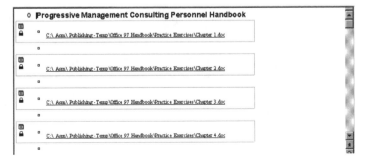

When the master document is collapsed, point to any subdocument and click to open it. When you want to return to the master document, just close and save the changes you made to the subdocument. You'll notice that the link to the subdocument changes color to show that you have already edited that document.

Subdocuments can only be opened for editing by one person at a time— if another person tries to open the same subdocument, they can only open a read-only copy. You can also lock people out from making changes to the master document or any subdocument by expanding the master document, selecting the document or documents you want to lock, and clicking the Lock Document button on the Master Document toolbar. This prevents anyone from making changes after a document is completed.

Creating a Master Document

1. Create a new document and click the Outline View button.

2. Enter the outline for the document, being careful to position each section at the same heading level.

3. Select a heading and text, and then click Create Subdocument on the Master Document toolbar.

4. Double-click any document icon in the top corner of the subdocument to open a subdocument.

5. Click the Collapse Subdocuments button to view only the subdocument names.

6. Select a document and click the Lock Document button to prevent other users from making changes to a subdocument.

7. Save the Master Document.

When the master document is expanded, you can work with it as if it were one document by just switching to Normal or Print Layout view. You can apply page numbering, headers and footers, a table of contents, an index, and references and adjust styles just as you would in a normal document.

Just make sure you're in the master document before making any of these changes, or you can easily have a real mess on your hands.

Converting Existing Documents and Making Changes

For a document to be converted to a master document, you must apply heading styles so you can work with it in Outline view. After you have applied heading styles, you can switch to Master Document view and follow the same steps you would to create a new master document. If you have several documents that you want to combine into one master document, you need to first create a new master document with a couple of (temporary, if need be) subdocuments.

 After you create the master document, move the insertion point to where you want to insert an existing document and click the Insert Subdocument button on the Master Document toolbar. You'll be taken to the Insert Subdocument dialog box where you can select the document you want to insert.

You can merge two subdocuments into one, split one subdocument into two, delete a subdocument, or convert a subdocument into master document text. Table 4.1 shows you how to accomplish these tasks.

T A B L E 4.1: Converting Subdocuments

Task	Action	Click
Merge two subdocuments	Select the two subdocuments	
Split one subdocument	Position insertion point at split point	
Delete a subdocument	Select the subdocument	Press the Delete key
Convert a subdocument to master document text	Select the subdocument	

Creating Master Documents from Existing Documents

1. Open the existing document and apply heading styles to the major sections of the document.

2. Click the Outline View button, and click the Create Subdocument button.

3. To insert another document, position the insertion point where you want the document inserted and click the Insert Subdocument button.

4. Save the master document.

Saving Multiple Versions of a Document

Objective W2000E.7.3

Whether you're working with a master document or an isolated document, you can save multiple versions of a document within the document itself and switch back and forth between versions.

To save a version, choose File ➤ Save As, and in the Save As dialog box, click the Tools button. Click Save Versions to open the Save Version dialog box. There you can enter comments describing this version for later reference.

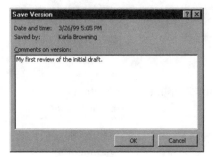

To view or switch between saved versions, choose File ➤ Versions. This dialog box allows you to open a different version, to delete a version that is no longer relevant, and to view comments about a version:

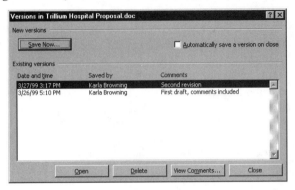

You can enable the Automatically Save a Version on Close check box to ensure that a version is preserved every time the document is edited. This option is particularly helpful when the document will be edited by several people consecutively. Although the most recently saved version will open by default, you can always go back to a previous version.

Saving Versions of a Document

1. Click the Save Versions button in the Save As dialog box.

2. Enter comments about the version you are saving. Click OK.

3. Choose File ➤ Versions to view a list of saved versions, to open or delete versions, to view comments, or to create an automatic version each time the document is closed.

Word 2000 only saves the changes in each version, but this can still result in slowing down your document's performance if there are several versions of a long document that contain lots of editing. If your document becomes too large, open the Versions dialog box and delete versions that you no longer need.

Tracking Changes to a Document

Objective W2000E.7.4

Although saving each version of a document is helpful, it's still difficult to identify where all the changes were made. Word 2000 will track each change to a document and allow you to accept or reject individual revisions or all revisions in one fell swoop. The easiest way to begin tracking changes is to right-click the dimmed option TRK on the status bar.

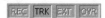

You can track changes in three ways:

- In the background with no visible queues
- On the screen
- In the printed document

To indicate which option you want, choose Highlight Changes from the pop-up menu. Choose Track Changes While Editing to turn on tracking. Then indicate whether you want the changes visible on the screen or in the printed document.

Clear both check boxes if you don't want the changes to be visible in either place. Click OK to close the dialog box and initiate tracking. You'll notice that TRK on the status bar is now enabled. If you choose to have changes visible on the screen, your documents will include a trail of every change. Text you insert will be a different color and will be underlined. Text you delete will be struck through. A vertical line in the margin will indicate lines where text has been changed. Figure 4.17 shows a document that has been edited with Highlight Changes on Screen turned on.

F I G U R E 4.17: Tracking changes in a document

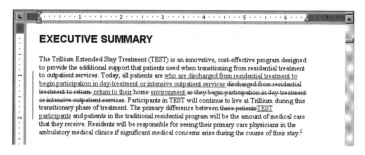

As other people open the document, changes they make will appear in different colors (as many 16 authors can work on one document before colors repeat). If you would prefer that all inserted text appear in one color and all deleted text in another, you can set the colors yourself by choosing Options from the pop-up menu or the Highlight Changes dialog box. The Track Changes dialog box lets you set color options for Inserted Text, Deleted Text, Changed Formatting, and Changed Lines.

Tracking Changes to a Document

1. Right-click TRK on the status bar (or choose Tools ➤ Track Changes) and choose Highlight Changes.

2. Click the Track Changes While Editing check box and choose whether to highlight changes on-screen and/or highlight changes in the printed document.

3. Click Options if you want to set a specific color for each type of revision—inserting, deleting, formatting, and borders.

4. When Tracking Changes is turned on, the status bar indicator is black. Double-click it to turn tracking off; double-click it again to turn tracking back on.

Accepting or Rejecting Changes

After a document has been edited, you can accept or reject changes. Right-click the status bar TRK indicator and choose Accept or Reject Changes.

The Accept or Reject Changes dialog box allows you to scroll through each individual change and accept or reject them as a group or individually:

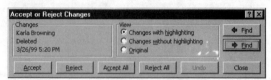

If you want to accept or reject all the changes without reviewing them, click the Accept All or Reject All button. Word will ask if you are certain—click Yes to confirm your choice.

 If, on the other hand, you want to review each individual revision, click Find to move through the document. Revisions will be selected one at a time, and you can choose to accept or reject each one. Word starts reviewing where the insertion point is currently located, so if you reach the end of the document without having gone through all the changes, Word will ask if you want to go to the beginning to catch the rest of them. It will also tell you when you have reviewed all the revisions. Click OK and then click Close to close the Accept or Reject Changes dialog box. If you don't want any more marked revisions, make sure you turn off tracking.

Accepting or Rejecting Changes

1. Right-click the status bar TRK indicator (or choose Tools ➤ Track Changes) and choose Accept or Reject Changes.

2. Click Accept All or Reject All if you don't want to review individual changes.

3. Click Find to review changes one by one. Word will select the change—click the Accept or Reject button and click Find again to move on to the next change.

4. Click Undo to reverse an accept or reject decision that you made.

5. Click Close to exit the Accept or Reject Changes dialog box. Remember to turn off tracking if you do not want further changes tracked.

Inserting Comments

> *Objective W2000E.7.1*

When you're creating or editing a document with others, it's often valuable to be able to make comments that aren't part of the printed document but can be viewed on-screen. Word's Comments feature fits the bill. You can insert comments, view comments from one or all reviewers, and print the comments.

To insert a comment, move the insertion point to where you want to position the comment and choose Insert ➤ Comment. The word immediately preceding the insertion point is highlighted, and your initials and a comment number appear in the text. A comment box then opens at the bottom of the screen.

Enter your comment and click Close. To view the comment, just hover over the highlighted word for a second—the insertion point will change to an I-beam with a note attached, and a second later the comment will appear above the text.

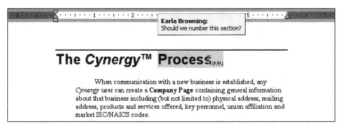

If you're going to be working a lot with comments, turn on the Reviewing toolbar, which includes buttons to insert, edit, and delete a comment and to move to previous and next comments.

Using Comments

1. Click where you want the comment to be inserted and choose Insert ➤ Comment.

2. Type your comment in the Comment box and click Close when you are finished.

3. Point to the comment to view it.

4. Turn on the Reviewing toolbar (choose View ➤ Toolbars ➤ Reviewing) to move between, edit, or delete comments.

5. To print the comments, choose File ➤ Print and choose Comments from the Print What drop-down list.

Protecting Documents

Objective W2000E.7.2

Although you may not think that there is much in your documents that anybody else would want, the sad truth is that your documents could become victims of corporate espionage or of unscrupulous colleagues out to pass your work off as their own. Add to that the risk that some well-meaning but misguided individual might revise one of your documents without your consent, and it's clear that it never hurts to be too careful.

Word 2000 provides several ways to protect your documents. You can:

▪ Restrict the access of anyone who doesn't have the password to open the document

▪ Require users to open read-only copies

▪ Recommend that users open the document as read-only so that, if they make changes, they must save it using a different name

▪ Prevent changes to a document you route for review, except for comments or tracked changes

To apply document protection, open the Save As dialog box. Click the Tools button and from the drop-down list choose General Options to open the Save dialog box. You can also access this page by choosing Tools ➣ Options and clicking the Save tab.

When you enable the Password to Open control, users will be prompted to input the password. Without the password, they will not be able to open the document.

If they know the password, the document will open, and they can modify it and save the changes. If they do not know the password, the document will not open and they are told why.

If you want users to be able to view but not change the original document, enter a Password to Modify. Users who don't know the password can only open the document as read-only and must save any changes under a different name. Click the Read-Only Recommended check box if you want to remind yourself or others that this document should not be modified and that it would be preferable to open it as read-only.

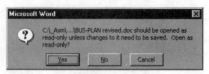

Whichever password option you choose, the password will not be visible on the screen as you type—Word will ask you to reenter the password for verification. Word then gives you a stern warning that password-protected documents cannot be opened if you forget the password. Take this warning seriously. If you forget the password for a document, it's gone for good. To change or delete a password, open the document and reenter or delete the password from the Save dialog box.

Protecting Document with Passwords

1. In the Save As dialog box, click the Tools button and choose General Options to open the Save dialog box, or choose Tools ➤ Options and click the Save tab.

2. Enter a Password to Open if you want users to be unable to open the document without a password. Click OK and reenter the password to confirm it. Click OK again and save the document.

3. Enter a Password to Modify if you want to allow all users to open the document as read-only but require a password to modify the original document. Click OK and reenter the password to confirm it. Click OK again and save the document.

4. Click the Read-Only Recommended check box if you want to suggest to users that they open the document as read-only to prevent accidental changes to an original document. Click OK and save the document.

5. To change or delete a password, open the document with the password, go to the Save dialog box, and enter a new password or delete the existing one.

Sending a Document via E-Mail

Objective W2000.4.10

Office 2000 makes sending a Word document via e-mail as easy as saving a document to a hard drive. You have three options for sending an e-mail message from Word. You can:

- Use Word as your Microsoft Outlook e-mail editor by choosing New ➤ Mail Message from Word's New menu
- Send a Word document from Word as the body of an e-mail message
- Send a document as an attachment by opening the document and choosing File ➤ Send To ➤ Mail Recipient as Attachment

With the first two options, an e-mail header opens at the top of the Word document. In this header, you can fill in To, CC, and Subject boxes, and set message options including importance, voting, tracking, and delivery options. When you are ready to send the message, click the Send or Send a Copy button. When you choose the attachment option, an e-mail message form opens with an icon for the document. Complete the e-mail message form and click Send to send the message.

NOTE   To use Word's e-mail options, you must have an e-mail service such as Outlook, Outlook Express, or Microsoft Exchange set up on your computer and have either a network connection or an Internet service provider.

Hands On

Objective W2000E.2.9, E.7.3, E.7.4, E.7.1, E.7.2, and 4.10

1. Create a master document using a newly created outline for a project you are working on. Be sure to apply the Heading style to each major topic before creating the subdocuments.

   a) Save the master document and collapse it.

b) Edit one of the subdocuments, close, and save it. Expand the master document and view the edited document.

c) Insert a new document into the master document. In the master document, edit and save changes to the inserted document.

d) Select and delete a subdocument from the master document.

e) Save and close the master document and any open subdocuments.

2. Open an existing document:

a) Turn on Track Changes. Make the changes visible on the screen.

b) Make changes to the document, inserting and deleting text. Save a version of the document. Make additional changes to the document and save another version.

c) Insert a comment and highlight some important text.

d) Protect the document for Tracked Changes or password protect it as read-only, then save another version of the document. Turn on Automatically Save Version on Close.

e) If you're on a network, or you have an Internet Service Provider, send this document to someone in your e-mail address book.

f) Open the Versions dialog box and view the Existing Versions. Close the Versions dialog box. Using Accept or Reject Changes, review each change made to the document and accept or reject each as you deem appropriate. Turn off Track Changes and save the final version.

CHAPTER

5

Working with Objects and Graphics

Too often a well-written document is overlooked because it simply isn't eye-catching enough to cause the reader to take a second glance. You can avoid this potential downfall with Word's object and graphic tools. Spice up text-heavy documents with a quote displayed in a nicely formatted text box. Give your statistics brand new life by creating charts to display them. Insert clip art and pictures into less formal documents to grab the attention of your reader and make your message a memorable one.

Converting, Linking, and Embedding in Word

An *object* is data that can be embedded or linked in another application. Object Linking and Embedding, or *OLE*, is a protocol that allows applications to communicate with each other to create or update objects. Pictures, charts, Excel worksheets, Access tables, and PowerPoint slides are all examples of objects you can convert, embed, or link in Word 2000 documents. As you'll see, you can also embed or link graphics, sounds, video, and virtually anything else you can select and copy to the clipboard.

The easiest way to convert, embed, or link data in Word uses a modification of copy-and-paste operations. Open the *source application* (also called the *native application*) that contains the text, picture, or other object you want to embed or link in the *destination application*. Select and copy the object to the clipboard. You can close the source application if you wish. In some programs, you'll be asked if you want to retain the contents of the clipboard; in this case, choose Yes. Then open the destination document and place the insertion point where you want to paste the selection. Choose Edit ➤ Paste Special to open the Paste Special dialog box, shown in Figure 5.1, where a range from an Excel worksheet is being pasted into a Word document.

F I G U R E 5.1: Paste Special dialog box

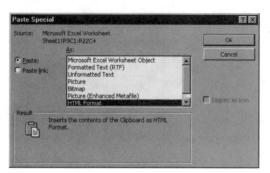

You choose to convert, embed, or link the selection in the destination application, depending on how you want to use the selection after it arrives. *Converting* the selection changes it from its native format to a format used in the destination document. For example, an Excel chart pasted in Word can be converted to a graphic or text. From the time of conversion, you'll use Word's tools to work with the converted selection. If you *embed* the chart object, a *copy* of the object that retains its native format is saved within the destination document. If you double-click an Excel object to edit it, the Excel toolbars open.

Objective W2000E.3.3

With a *link*, each time you open the destination document, the application reloads the object from its native application file. If you double-click to edit the linked object, the source document opens; you can't change the linked object, only its source. If a linked file is moved or renamed, opening the destination document results in an error message and the destination document loads without the linked object. This means you can only successfully open the document on a computer that contains both the native application and the source document. Linking has two advantages: it saves disk space, but, more importantly, linking is *dynamic*. If the object's source changes, the change is reflected in all linked documents.

The source for the object is displayed at the top of the dialog box (see Figure 5.1). The As box allows you to select how the information should be pasted:

- Microsoft Excel Worksheet Object creates an embedded Excel object in the Word document you can edit using regular Excel tools.

- Formatted Text (RTF) converts the worksheet to a table.

- Unformatted Text converts the selection to Word tabular columns.

- Picture and Bitmap both convert the worksheet into a graphic you can work with in Word using all the Word graphics tools.

- Picture (Enhanced Metafile) converts the selection into a Windows Metafile graphic.

- HTML, the default, inserts the contents of the clipboard as HTML-formatted text.

- Unformatted Unicode Text inserts the worksheet without any formatting.

Microsoft Excel Worksheet

If you chose the Microsoft Excel Worksheet Object option, you can click the Display As Icon check box to insert an icon rather than text. If you prefer to change the type of Excel Worksheet Object icon, click the Change Icon button in the Paste Special dialog box. You can choose from Excel's icon library or import your own using the Browse button, and you can customize the caption as well.

To link (rather than to embed) the selection, choose the Paste Link option. You can link any of the converted file types listed except for Enhanced Metafile. The Enhanced Metafile option is replaced with Word Hyperlink. Choosing Word Hyperlink creates a hyperlink in the Word document; clicking the hyperlink takes the user to the source Excel worksheet. You can access the Paste as Hyperlink option directly from the Edit menu.

Converting, Embedding, and Linking an Excel Spreadsheet

1. Open the file that contains the data to be converted, embedded, or linked.

2. Select the data and copy the selection to the clipboard.

3. Open the destination document.

4. Place the insertion point where you want to paste the selection.

5. Choose Edit ➤ Paste Special.

**Converting, Embedding, and Linking an
Excel Spreadsheet** *(continued)*

6. Select a type from the As control. Choose Paste or Paste Link.

7. Select the Display As Icon option if you are choosing a Microsoft Excel Worksheet Object.

8. Click OK to paste the selection in the destination document.

NOTE   From the computer's point of view, OLE is a complex operation. Give the destination document a moment to accept and place the new object.

▶ *Objective W2000E.3.4*

Click the pasted object once to select it. Use the object's handles to size it, or click Delete to delete it. The real magic of OLE occurs when you double-click the object. After you click, wait a moment. If the object was embedded, the toolbars from the object's native application open in the destination application. The embedded object is a copy. Changing the object doesn't change the original worksheet, and changes in the source worksheet have no effect on the object. With a linked object, double-click and you'll be transported to the source document to edit the object.

OLE Using PowerPoint, Access, and Outlook

PowerPoint creates slide and presentation objects, which can be embedded in Word documents. Convert, embed, or link a PowerPoint slide just as you did with the Excel worksheet. Copy the slide in PowerPoint, then switch to Word and click at the destination location. Choose Edit ➤ Paste Special to adjust the settings in the dialog box. PowerPoint also accepts embedded objects from Word and Excel if you want to go the other way.

OLE requires a source application that can create an OLE object (an *OLE server*) and a destination application that can accept OLE objects (an *OLE client*). Access and Outlook are OLE clients, but not OLE servers, so they cannot create OLE objects. You can paste Access tables, fields, or records and Outlook items in Word, but the result is a Word table, not an object. Selections pasted from Access and Outlook can't be linked. As OLE clients, Access and Outlook accept objects from other applications. You can embed part of a document from Word in an Access form or report or Outlook item.

OLE with Files

If you want to embed or link an entire file instead of a selection, it is often easier to insert the object. Choose Insert ➤ Object ➤ Create from File to open the Create from File page of the Object dialog box, shown in Figure 5.2.

F I G U R E 5.2: Create from File page of the Object dialog box

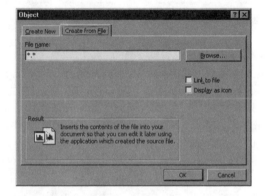

Select and open the file you want to embed or link, and then set the other options as you did in the Paste Special dialog box. Click OK to insert the object in the destination document. Some files are inserted as icons, whether or not you choose Display As Icon. Sound files, for example, place an icon in the destination document. Double-clicking the icon plays the sound file.

Embedding or Linking a File

1. Open the destination document and place the insertion point where the object is to be inserted.

2. Choose Insert ➤ Object from the menu. Click the Create from File tab.

Embedding or Linking a File *(continued)*

3. Browse to select the file you want to embed or link.

4. Click the OK button to embed the file, or choose Link to File, and then click OK to link the file.

Creating New Objects

You can use the Object dialog box to create a new object. For example, you might want to have an Excel worksheet in a Word document. You don't have to open Excel and create the worksheet; you can create an Excel worksheet object in Word. Because new objects don't exist as separate source files, they cannot be linked, only embedded.

Office 2000 includes other programs—such as Microsoft Publisher—that are OLE servers. You probably have other non-Office applications on your computer that also create objects. Choosing Insert ➤ Object from the menu opens the Object dialog box. The scroll list on the Create New page displays the objects that can be created using applications installed on your computer, as shown in Figure 5.3.

F I G U R E 5.3: Creating a new object

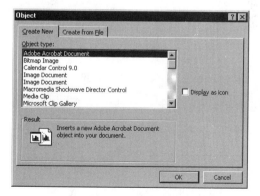

Select an Object Type and then click OK. The appropriate OLE server opens within the current document. Create the object, then click in the destination document (outside the object) to close the OLE server.

Creating a New Object

1. Position the insertion point in the document and choose Insert ➤ Object from the menu bar.

2. Click the Create New tab. Select an Object Type from the scroll list.

3. Click the OK button to insert the newly-created object.

The Object Type list is amended as new applications are installed. Applications may remain on the list even if they have been removed from the computer. If you select an application that has been moved or removed, the destination application provides an error message.

Hands On

Objectives W2000E.3.1, E.3.3, and E.3.4

1. Create or open an Excel worksheet. Select and copy a range of cells and place them in a Word document as

   a) A converted table using Paste

   b) A picture using Paste Special

   c) An embedded Excel object using Paste Special

   d) A linked Excel worksheet object

   e) A linked picture

2. Double-click either of the linked objects, and make changes to the Excel worksheet. Return to the Word document and notice the differences between the converted, embedded, and linked objects.

3. Place a sound or video file in Word using Insert ➤ Object ➤ Create from File. Play the media file.

Inserting Clips and Other Graphics

If you're thinking of clip art as being too "cutesy" for the office, think again! With hundreds of clips from which to choose, you're sure to find the right piece of art to enhance your message in a professional way. The company newsletter might be a good place to try a few carefully selected, well-placed graphics. Begin by choosing Insert from the menu. If the type of media you want to insert is listed on the Insert menu, select it. If not, choose Object and select the media type from the list in the Insert Object dialog box.

Adding Clips to a Word Document

▶ Objective W2000.6.2

The Microsoft Clip Gallery, included with Office 2000, has a broad selection of media clips. When you add other media files to your system, you can add them to the gallery for easy selection. Click Insert ➢ Picture ➢ ClipArt to open the Insert ClipArt dialog box, as shown in Figure 5.4.

F I G U R E 5.4: Microsoft Clip Gallery

Even though the Insert menu choice says ClipArt, you can insert any of the files in the Gallery. It's probably faster to insert ClipArt, and then choose a sound or video clip, than to insert a sound or video object in the Insert Object dialog box.

The Clip Gallery is arranged in categories. Click one of the icons displayed in the gallery to choose a category. Once a category choice is made, locate the thumbnail for the clip you want to insert.

Not all clips in a category are displayed at once. If you wish to see additional clips, click Keep Looking at the bottom of the scroll list. Shift+Backspace also displays more clips when the Clip Gallery is open. Continue to choose Keep Looking until you locate the exact clip you are looking for.

Once you are several layers deep in the Clip Gallery, you can use the Back and Forward buttons at the top of the dialog box to navigate between current and previous screens.

Click the object once to select it and open a shortcut toolbar with choices to Insert the ClipArt, Preview the ClipArt, Add the clip to a Category, or Search for similar clips.

Choosing the Preview option enlarges the thumbnail so you can see more detail. Close the preview and choose Insert Clip if you decide you like it. You may decide to put this clip in another category. Choosing the third option on the shortcut toolbar allows you to reference the clip in an additional category you select from a list.

The Find option allows you to search for similar clips. You have the option of searching for clips by Artistic Style, Color and Shape or key word. Click one of the buttons or click a key word to move to a page of similar clips.

Your search history is kept on a drop-down list at the top of the Insert ClipArt dialog box. If you wish to duplicate a past search, simply choose the key word from the list and press Enter to perform that search again.

 When you choose Add to Category or Search for Similar Clips, the pane that opens stays in view unless you click the Hide Pane button at the top-right corner of the dialog box.

You can choose to insert multiple clips at one time, since the Gallery stays open until you close it and return to your Word document. If you change your mind and wish to delete a clip, click it once to select it then press Delete on your keyboard.

Inserting Clips from the Clip Gallery

1. Position the insertion point where you want to insert the clip.

2. Choose Insert ➤ Picture ➤ ClipArt to open the Clip Gallery.

3. Click the file-type tab to browse Pictures, Sound, or Motion Clips. Select a category and use the scroll bar to see thumbnails of clips.

4. Preview a picture by clicking it and then clicking the Preview icon on the shortcut toolbar. With video and sound clips, select one and click the Play Clip icon to see a preview.

5. Choose a clip, then click Insert on the shortcut toolbar or double-click the sound, video, clip art, or picture to add it to the document.

6. Delete clip art by selecting it and pressing Delete.

Once you insert a clip, you can usually resize or otherwise edit it. See "Grouping and Ungrouping Objects" for information on editing clip art.

Importing Clips

If your company has a logo or other clip art you want to import into Word, you can use the Import Clips feature in the Clip Gallery window to store them in an easily accessible place.

To import clips from other locations, click the Import Clips button to open the Add Clip to Clip Gallery dialog box shown in Figure 5.5. Search for the art with the Look In drop-down list or choose the last option in the Clip Import Option control—this lets the Clip Gallery locate and import the art on its own. You can import a copy of the new clip art by selecting Copy into Clip Gallery or you can move the original by selecting Move into Clip Gallery.

F I G U R E 5.5: Importing a clip

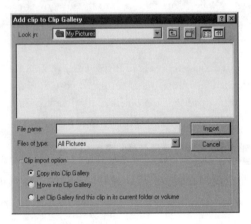

You can also import new clips directly from the Web by clicking the Clips Online button in the Insert ClipArt dialog box. Internet Explorer takes you to Microsoft's online Clip Art Gallery, provided you are already online. Search a Web site for additional clip art to be imported to the Clip Gallery.

Moving and Resizing Clips

Objective W2000E.4.2

To move a selected clip, drag it with the mouse. You can also drag the clip's handle to resize the clip. Although you can resize a video clip as you can any other object by dragging a sizing handle, be aware that badly-resized video is blurry, difficult to see, and sometimes skips during playback. Delete any clip by selecting it and pressing Delete on the keyboard.

TIP It is often easier to move a clip after you've set the text wrapping options. See "Using Advanced Text Alignment Features" later in this chapter.

Inserting Other Pictures

Objective W2000E.4.1

If the picture you want to insert isn't in the Clip Gallery, choose Insert ➤ Picture ➤ From File to open the Insert Picture dialog box, shown below.

The default is to look for all picture files when you open the Insert Picture dialog box. If you're searching for one particular picture type—bitmaps, for instance—then change the Files of Type drop-down to indicate that picture file type. Locate and select the picture file you want, and then click the Insert button to close the dialog box and place the graphic in your document.

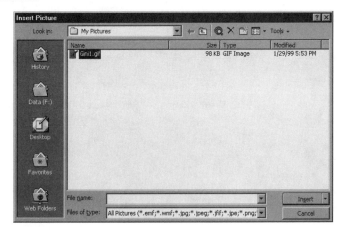

TIP   To see a picture before you insert it, switch to Preview from the View drop-down list in the Insert Picture dialog box.

Modifying Pictures

After you've placed a picture from a file or the Clip Gallery, you can adjust the picture using the Picture toolbar. Right-click the picture and choose Show Picture Toolbar from the shortcut menu. (If Hide Picture Toolbar is an option on the shortcut menu, the toolbar is already turned on.) Table 5.1 describes the buttons on the Picture toolbar.

T A B L E 5.1: Picture Toolbar Buttons

Button	Name	Use
	Insert Picture	Insert another picture from a location you specify
	Image Control	Choose from Automatic, Grayscale, Black & White, or Watermark
	More Contrast	Increase color intensity
	Less Contrast	Decrease color intensity
	More Brightness	Add white to lighten the colors
	Less Brightness	Add black to darken the colors
	Crop	Trim rectangular areas from the image
	Line Style	Format the border that surrounds the picture
	Text Wrapping	Allows you to choose if and how text wraps
	Object/Format	One-stop shopping for picture properties
	Set Transparent Color	Used like an eyedropper to make areas of the picture transparent; used extensively for Web graphics
	Reset Picture	Return the picture to its original format

The Crop, Recolor Picture, and Set Transparent Color buttons are used with areas of the picture. All other buttons affect the entire picture.

Inserting Scanned Graphics

If your computer is hooked to a scanner, you can scan images into Word through the Microsoft Photo Editor. Choose Insert ➤ Picture ➤ From Scanner or Camera, and the Photo Editor launches. You are required to set some scanner options; the actual options vary for different scanner models.

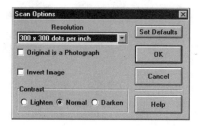

Make sure the document you want to scan is in the scanner, and then click OK. After the image scans, you can alter it in the Photo Editor. (See the Photo Editor's online Help for more information.) When you close the Photo Editor, the image is placed in your Word document.

Using Advanced Text Alignment Features

Objective W2000E.6.6

When you insert a picture into a document that contains text, the text automatically moves out of the way and lets the picture have center stage. To change the text wrapping options, right-click on the picture and choose Format Picture. Click the Layout tab to access the text wrapping and alignment properties. You have a choice of five wrapping styles: In Line with Text, Square, Tight, Behind Text, and In Front of Text and four alignments: Left, Center, Right, and Other.

Choose Other and click the Advanced tab if you want so specify a more exact picture position and other wrapping options. The Picture Position tab lets you indicate specific Horizontal and Vertical positions for the picture. The Text Wrapping tab gives you additional wrapping style choices and allows you to identify whether you want the text to wrapping on Both

Sides, Left Only, Right Only, or Largest Only. You can also indicate how close the picture should be to the text on the Top, Bottom, Left, and Right.

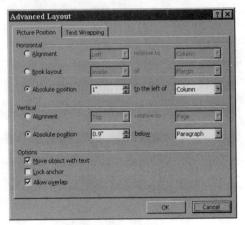

Hands On

Objectives W2000.6.2, E.4.1, E.4.2, and E.6.6

1. Start Word with a blank document or open an existing document.

   a) Insert clip art from the Clip Gallery.

   b) Size and position the clip.

   c) Insert a video or sound clip.

   d) Play the clip.

2. Open the Clip Gallery.

   a) Download a picture from the Microsoft online Clip Gallery.

   b) Insert the downloaded picture into a document.

   c) Use the tools on the Picture toolbar to retouch the picture.

   d) Select and delete the picture.

3. Insert clip art from the Clip Gallery into a document with existing text.

   a) Open the Picture toolbar and use the Set Transparent Color tool to make part of the clip (like the background) transparent.

   b) Change the text wrapping to Square and view the results.

   c) Wrap text only on the left side of the picture and increase the Left and Right distance from the text to .15. View the results.

4. Insert a bitmap image into a new or existing Word document. Move and resize the image, then experiment with text wrapping options.

Doing It Yourself with Draw

Microsoft Draw is a built-in Office application that lets you create line art and other objects, such as WordArt. In Word, you could create your own graphics two ways. You might choose to begin by choosing Insert ➤ Picture ➤ New Drawing or Insert ➤ Object and choosing a Microsoft Draw object in the dialog box. The new object is placed on a separate layer in front of the document. While working with the object, you'll have access to all the available drawing tools, including the Drawing toolbar. When you complete your drawing, simply click outside the object's frame to return to the document layer.

Objective W2000.6.1

It's probably easier and more efficient to start with the Drawing toolbar and use those tools to create your own graphics. Access the Drawing toolbar as you would any other toolbar: right-click a toolbar or choose View ➤ Toolbars.

 In Word you have an additional option for activating the Drawing toolbar: click the Drawing button on the Standard toolbar.

The Drawing toolbar includes two broad categories of menus and buttons. The first set, beginning with AutoShapes and ending with WordArt, is used to create drawing objects. The buttons to the right of WordArt are used to format existing objects.

Inserting AutoShapes

Clicking the AutoShapes button opens a list of AutoShape categories:

Choose a category, and a menu of AutoShapes opens. Select an AutoShape by clicking it, and then click or drag to insert the shape in the document. If you intend to add a lot of AutoShapes (for example, when creating a flow chart), you can drag the bar at the top of the menu and place the menu in the document as a freestanding toolbar.

TIP   Callout AutoShapes are used for annotating other objects or elements, so when you place a callout, the insertion point automatically appears. To place text in any other AutoShape, right-click the AutoShape and choose Add Text.

Inserting Line Art Objects

To draw a line or arrow, click the Line button or the Arrow button. Move the crosshair pointer to one end of the line you want to draw. Hold the mouse button and drag to draw the line. Release the button to create the line and turn the Line or Arrow tool off. (With the Arrow tool, the arrowhead appears at the end of the line where you released the mouse button.) If you want a line that is absolutely horizontal or vertical in relation to the page, hold the Shift key while dragging the line. The Line and other object buttons work like the Format Painter button: When you have more than one object to draw, begin by double-clicking its button. The button stays depressed, allowing you to draw more objects, until you click any button.

With the Rectangle and Oval buttons, drag from one corner of the object to the opposite corner, then release the mouse button. Hold the Shift key while dragging to create circular ovals or square rectangles.

TIP   If you need a series of identical objects, create one object, and then use copy and paste.

Use the Text Box tool to create text that floats on a layer above standard document text. Draw the text box as you would a rectangle. When you release the mouse button, an insertion point appears in the text box. Select and format the text using the Formatting toolbar.

Adding Drawing Objects

1. If the Drawing toolbar is not on, right-click any toolbar and select Drawing from the list, or click the Drawing button on the Standard toolbar.

2. Choose an AutoShape category and shape from the AutoShapes menu, or click any of the drawing tools in the first cluster of buttons to change the pointer to crosshairs for drawing lines and shapes. Double-click the tool to draw more than one object.

3. Drag the crosshairs from a starting point to the point where you want the line or shape to end. Hold the Shift key while dragging to create straight lines, round ovals, or square rectangles.

4. Release the mouse button to end the line or shape and to turn off a tool you selected with a single click. Click another drawing button to turn off a tool you selected with a double click.

Adding WordArt

WordArt is used to create a graphic object from text. You'll use WordArt to create logos, emphasize titles, and add excitement to a document.

 To create WordArt, place the insertion point where you want the graphic, and click the WordArt button on the Drawing toolbar to open the WordArt Gallery, shown in Figure 5.6.

FIGURE 5.6: WordArt Gallery

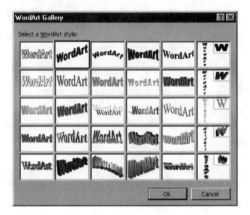

In the Gallery, select a WordArt style and click OK. (You can select a different style at any time.) When the Edit WordArt Text dialog box opens, enter the text you wish to create WordArt from. Use the Font and Size drop-downs and Bold and Italics buttons to format the text. Click OK to place the WordArt object in your document and open the WordArt toolbar. The toolbar buttons are described in Table 5.2.

TABLE 5.2: WordArt Toolbar Buttons

Button	Name	Use
	Insert WordArt	Creates a new WordArt object.
	Edit Text	Opens Edit WordArt Text dialog box to edit text.
	WordArt Gallery	Opens WordArt Gallery.
	Format WordArt	Opens Format WordArt dialog box so you can format colors, position, and wrap properties.

T A B L E 5.2: WordArt Toolbar Buttons *(continued)*

Button	Name	Use
	WordArt Shape	Opens a Shape menu so you can select the basic shape into which the text should be poured.
	Free Rotate	Changes object handles to rotation handles so you can rotate text. Click again to turn off.
	Same Letter Heights	Makes all letters the same height, irrespective of case.
	Vertical Text	Changes WordArt orientation from horizontal to vertical. Click again to reverse.
	Alignment	Opens an alignment menu with standard options and unique WordArt options.
	Character Spacing	Opens an adjustment menu so you can change space between characters.

Use the WordArt toolbar buttons or the Drawing toolbar buttons (see the next section, "Formatting Objects") to enhance the WordArt object.

Creating WordArt

1. Place the insertion point where you want the WordArt to appear.

2. Click the WordArt button on the Drawing toolbar.

3. Select a style from the WordArt Gallery and click OK.

4. Type the text you want to convert to WordArt in the Edit WordArt Text dialog box. Change fonts, font sizes, and styles as desired, then click OK.

5. Use the WordArt toolbar buttons to format the WordArt object.

Formatting Objects

Use the Drawing toolbar's formatting buttons to format selected objects, including WordArt. To select a single object, just click it.

To select multiple objects, either hold Shift while clicking each object, or use the Select Objects tool and drag a rectangle around the objects you want to select.

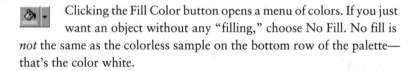

Clicking the Fill Color button opens a menu of colors. If you just want an object without any "filling," choose No Fill. No fill is *not* the same as the colorless sample on the bottom row of the palette—that's the color white.

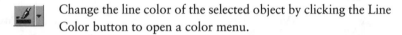

Change the line color of the selected object by clicking the Line Color button to open a color menu.

The Font Color button changes the text color in a selected object like a text box or callout. With all three color buttons, if there is no object selected, the color you choose is the new default color and is applied to objects you create in the future.

The Line Style button opens a line style menu. Selecting More Lines from the menu opens a Format AutoShape dialog box, where you can set other line widths and object attributes.

The Dash Style menu includes solid lines, dotted lines, dashed lines, and other combinations thereof.

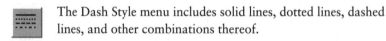

In the Arrow Style menu, select the style that should appear at the ends of the selected line from arrowheads and terminators of various types. If the combination of line endings you desire isn't in the menu, choose More Arrows to open the Format dialog box and set a beginning and ending style for the line.

Special Shadow and 3-D Effects

Shadow and 3-D effects are designed to give the selected drawing object more depth. You must choose one or the other; if you apply a 3-D effect to a shadowed object, the shadow is removed, and vice versa.

From the Shadow menu, you can choose a shadow style for the selected object. To format the shadow, choose Shadow Settings from the Shadow menu to open the Shadow Settings toolbar. The toolbar includes buttons to nudge the shadow up, down, left, or right, and a Shadow Color menu.

 You can add a 3-D effect to any object. With the options on the 3-D Settings toolbar, you can change the extrusion (depth) of the object as well as rotation, perspective angle, lighting direction, surface texture, and color. When you change the color of a 3-D effect, the change affects only the effect, not the object itself.

Arranging Objects

The Draw menu on the Drawing toolbar includes other options for manipulating objects. Drawing objects are placed in separate *layers* on top of the text in a document. To move objects from layer to layer, choose Draw ➤ Order to open the Order menu.

Bring to Front and Send to Back move the selected object(s) in relation to text and other graphic objects. If you draw an oval and place a rectangle over the right half of it, the rectangle covers part of the oval. If you want the entire oval to show, covering part of the rectangle, either send the rectangle to the back or bring the oval to the front.

If you're working with more than two layers, use the Bring Forward and Send Backward buttons to move the selected objects one layer at a time.

Objective W2000E.2.5

If you want to print a document with a watermark, you need a graphic that is light in color so it doesn't overshadow the text in front of it. If the graphic you want to use is too dark, you can lighten it after you insert it into the document. To create a watermark, you have your choice of two methods:

1. Choose View ➤ Header and Footer. Click the Show/Hide Document Text button on the Header and Footer toolbar. Insert the graphic and reposition it on the page (it does not have to be contained in the Header area). Click Close to leave Header and Footer view.

2. Insert a graphic into the document. Choose Draw ➤ Order on the Drawing toolbar and click Send Behind Text.

With either method, you can lighten the graphic by right-clicking it (if you use the first method, you must switch to Header and Footer view again to right-click it) and choosing Format ➤ Picture. Click the Picture tab and change the Image control to Watermark. You may also want to adjust the Fill Color on the Color and Lines tab. If the watermark is still too dark when you print it, adjust the Brightness and Contrast controls on the Picture tab of the Format Picture dialog box.

NOTE   If you want to create a watermark that appears on every page of the document, use the Header and Footer option.

Ordering Objects

1. Select the object you want to bring forward or move back.

2. Click Draw (on the Drawing toolbar) and choose Order.

3. Choose Bring to Front, Send to Back, Bring Forward, or Send Backward to switch the position of one graphic relative to another.

4. Click the Bring in Front of Text or Send Behind Text button on the Drawing toolbar if you want to position text in relation to a graphic.

You can adjust individual objects in a drawing using the Nudge, Align and Distribute, and Rotate or Flip options on the Draw menu. If you're doing detailed work, consider turning on a grid (choose Draw ➤ Grid) to help you properly align various objects in the drawing.

Grouping and Ungrouping Objects

When your drawing is complete, you can *group* all the drawing objects so they are treated as a single object.

Select all the objects, then choose Draw ➤ Group from the Drawing toolbar. The handles on the multiple selected objects are replaced with one set of handles that can be used to size or move the entire object.

If an object contains more than one element, you can *ungroup* it into separate objects, each of which can be individually moved, sized, formatted,
or deleted. This is the easiest way to format clip art images. Ungroup the
image, then change fills and line colors, or delete portions of the image.
When you have finished editing, select all the objects and group them
again so you can move or size the entire image.

Creating Charts

In Office, there are two programs that create charts: Excel and Microsoft
Graph. If you already have a chart in Excel, you can easily copy it and
embed or link it to your document. However, if you don't have access to
Excel, Microsoft Graph lets you create charts quickly and easily in Word.

Creating Charts

Objective W2000E.4.3

To launch Microsoft Graph, choose Insert ➤ Object from the menu, then
select Microsoft Graph 2000 Chart from the scroll list in the Object dialog box.

NOTE You can also access Microsoft Graph 2000 by choosing Insert ➤
Picture ➤ Chart.

In Figure 5.7, you can see that Graph contains two windows: a datasheet
that includes sample data, and a chart. Replace the labels (text) in the top
row and left column with your labels and the values in the remaining cells
with your numbers, and you have a basic bar chart. To delete a column
or row you don't need, click its header and press Delete. Close the
datasheet at any point to place the chart in your document.

You can resize and reposition the chart object as you would any other
object. You must select the chart to resize it; a selected chart object has
hollow handles. Double-clicking the chart opens the chart object so you
can edit the individual objects inside it; when you can edit the chart, the
object handles are solid, and you cannot move the chart object. To select

the entire object again for moving or sizing, click outside of the chart to close it, then click the chart object once.

When the chart is selected, you'll see additional chart tools appended to the Standard toolbar.

TIP If you're having difficulty moving the chart because you can't see the hollow handles, select it and format it for text wrapping. Text wrapping options are found on the Draw menu, which you can access from the Drawing toolbar.

FIGURE 5.7: Inserting a Microsoft Graph Chart object

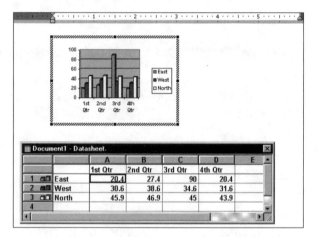

Using Existing Data

Objective W2000E.4.4

If you already have data, don't reenter it—you can import or copy data into Microsoft Graph. Graph can convert data from Excel, text files, SYLK files, Lotus 1-2-3, and CSV (comma separated files) that can be exported from most spreadsheet and database programs.

 To import data from an existing file, start Graph just as you would if you were creating a chart from scratch, choose Edit ➤ Import File on the Graph menu or click the Import File button to open the Import File dialog box. Once you choose a file in this typical Windows file selection window, the Import Data Options dialog box opens so you can select which part of the workbook or worksheet to use. Turn on Overwrite Existing Cells to replace the current data in the Graph datasheet. Turn this option off, and the imported data is appended at the end of the current data in the datasheet.

Copying or Linking Existing Data

Use Copy and Paste or Paste Special to use existing data from Word or Excel to create a chart. Select and copy the data in its source application. In the Graph datasheet, select the first cell where you want the data to appear. Choose the upper-left cell to overwrite the existing data, or select the left cell in an empty row to append the data. Paste the data, or choose Edit ➤ Paste Link from the Graph menu to link the chart to the table or worksheet. Remember, with linking, changes you make to the data in the source application are automatically reflected in the Graph chart.

If you often work in Excel, you probably create most of your charts there. However, you can choose to create charts from within Word using Microsoft Graph and have access to most of Excel's formatting features as well.

Formatting a Chart

Graph has buttons that append themselves to the Standard toolbar once a chart is created. You have all the features you'll need to create a great-looking representation of your numerical data. Table 5.3 describes the buttons on the Graph toolbar.

T A B L E 5.3: Microsoft Graph Toolbar Buttons

Button	Name	Use
	By Rows	Displays data series by row. First row of the table provides x-axis labels.
	By Columns	Displays data series by column. First column of the table provides x-axis labels.
	Data Table	Toggles between showing and hiding data table with chart.
	Chart Type	Allows you to change to another chart type such as 3-D Pie or Area.
	Category Axis Guidelines	Toggles to show or hide major vertical guidelines on chart.
	Value Axis Guidelines	Toggles to show or hide major horizontal guidelines on chart.
	Legend	Toggles to show or hide legend.
	Drawing	Turns Drawing toolbar off or on.
	Fill Color	Fills background of selected chart area.

You can hide the datasheet display using the View Datasheet button on the Graph toolbar. Turning the datasheet off won't prevent you from displaying it with the chart in your document; you can still use the Data Table button referred to in Table 5.3. However, to edit numbers in the datasheet, you must display it.

With the chart selected, right-click and choose Chart Options to open the Chart Options dialog box. Use the dialog box options to add titles, display minor as well as major gridlines, show and position a legend, display data labels, and include the datasheet as part of the chart object.

 To format an individual chart object (for example, the columns, all the data in a row or column, the chart background, or the legend), select the object in the chart, or choose it from the Chart Objects drop-down list on the toolbar. Then double-click the selected object, right-click and choose Format [Object Name], or click the Format Object button on the toolbar to open the relevant dialog box. As an example, the Format Data Series dialog box is shown in Figure 5.8.

WARNING When you select an entire data series for formatting and then double-click an item in the chart to open the Format dialog box, the formatting is *only* applied to whichever point in the data series you double-clicked. If you want to apply formatting to the entire data series, select it using any of the methods described above, and then open the Format dialog box using the toolbar button, rather than double-clicking the chart object.

Several options are available to you when you choose to format individual chart objects:

- Use the Patterns tab of the dialog box to change borders and shading of the selected chart objects.

- Use the Shape tab (when formatting a data series) for changing the shape of bars in your graph.

- You can display values or percents on point in a series using the Data Labels tab.

- Increase the depth of the chart and the space between each category of columns under Options.

When you've made all your choices, click OK.

F I G U R E 5.8: The Format Data Series dialog box

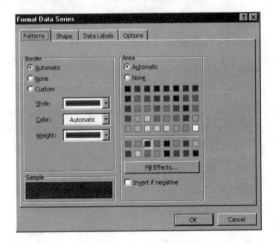

Hands On

Objectives W2000.6.1, 6.2, E.4.3, and E.4.4

1. Start a new Word document or open an existing document.

    a) Use the drawing tools to draw a simple picture that includes AutoShapes and lines.

    b) Use the formatting tools on the Drawing toolbar to format individual objects in the drawing.

    c) Select and group all the drawing objects.

    d) Create and format WordArt.

    e) Place an AutoShape.

    f) Apply 3-D effects to the AutoShape.

    g) Use the 3-D Settings toolbar to format the 3-D effects.

2. Create a chart using Microsoft Graph 2000.

    a) Overwrite the sample data in the datasheet with your own. Delete rows and columns you don't need.

    b) Format the chart so it shows both minor and major gridlines.

    c) Turn off the legend, then turn it back on again.

3. Create a new chart by importing data from an existing Excel worksheet.

    a) Delete rows and columns of data you don't need from the datasheet.

    b) Format the individual chart objects to your liking.

CHAPTER

6

Creating Web Pages in Word

Your supervisor has just asked you to create a series of Web pages for your corporate intranet. If you haven't created Web pages but have heard the lunchroom rumors about HTML, this new assignment can be pretty intimidating. Fear no more. Word 2000 is designed to put your anxiety to rest. All you need to do is add a few new skills to your bag of tricks, and you'll be producing dazzling pages in no time.

Starting a Web Page in Word

Word 2000 provides three ways to create Web pages:

- Using the Web Page wizard
- Applying a Web template
- Converting an existing Word document

The Web Page wizard not only creates Web pages but actually creates full Webs: collections of pages with links between them. If the project you are undertaking involves multiple documents, the Web Page wizard is generally the best choice because it creates links for you and gives your pages a consistent look and feel. If you are providing content to your corporate intranet and you've been given a template to use, you may want to apply the template directly or convert an existing document without going through the wizard. However, after you use the wizard, you'll find it's a great tool whatever your goal.

Creating Web Pages Using the Web Page Wizard

The Web Page wizard can create single pages or entire Webs. If you want to create more than one page, it's a good idea to draw up the layout of your Web before you start the wizard. You'll want to know the names of as many pages as possible so the wizard can create the links between them.

If you have existing documents you want to include in the Web, be sure to know their names and where to locate them. The wizard isn't included in the Typical Office installation, but can be automatically installed on demand, so make sure you have access to the CD or network drive from which Office was installed.

When you are ready to create your Web pages, click File ➤ New. Click the Web Pages tab in the New dialog box and select Web Page Wizard. Click OK to start the wizard and Next to move on to the first step.

The Title and Location page, as shown in Figure 6.1, determines the official title of your Web. Although it can be changed later, it's important to give your Web a descriptive title because the various Web search engines use the site's title when they search for a site on the Internet. A good title could mean the difference between someone finding your site or not.

By default, the wizard creates a new folder for your Web, so if you change the location be sure you change it to an empty folder. The wizard creates additional subfolders for storing graphics and other supporting files, but the main pages are stored in the folder you specify. If you don't designate a unique folder, your Web files will get mixed in with unrelated documents, making it difficult to manage the Web effectively. Enter the title and location and click Next.

F I G U R E 6.1: Title and Location

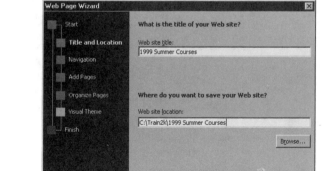

Using Frames for Navigation

The Web Page wizard offers three choices for the layout of your pages, as shown in Figure 6.2.

- A vertical frame runs down the left side of the page and contains links to the other pages in the Web.

- A horizontal frame is positioned across the top of the page and contains links to the other pages in the Web.

- The Separate Page option doesn't use frames; instead, each page opens in a full window. Forward and Back buttons and appropriate links are added to the pages.

Choose the Navigation option you prefer and click Next.

F I G U R E 6.2: Navigation types

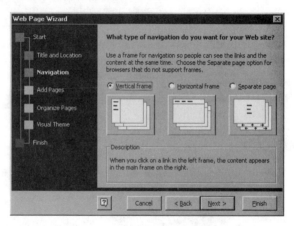

WARNING   Not all browsers support frames, and text readers, used by people with vision impairments, can't read pages with frames. Many Web developers who use frames also offer visitors a no-frame alternative on the site's Welcome page, but if you can only choose one layout, choose the Separate Page option for the widest range of accessibility.

Differentiating Text Frames from Web Frames

You may already be familiar with text frames for positioning text on a page. Text frames are used extensively in PowerPoint and Publisher and can be used in Word and Excel to position a block of text outside of the normal paragraphs or cells. Web frames also may contain text, but their primary purpose is to organize content on a Web page. Web frames typically appear on the top or left of a page and include navigational links that remain visible even when the visitor moves to a different page of your Web. See "Working with Frames" later in this chapter for more information.

Adding Pages

A Web created by the Web Page wizard comes with three pages: a Personal Web Page and two blank pages. The Personal Web Page is a template that includes sections for work information, favorite links, contact information, current projects, biographical information, and personal interests. If you are not creating a personal Web with you as the focus, you can delete this page by selecting it and clicking Remove Page. The first blank page moves into position as the new home page for your Web.

NOTE   The home page is typically the first page a visitor sees when they visit a Web site, but it may be preceded by a Welcome page that gives visitors options such as no frames or no graphics.

If you want to add additional pages to your Web, now is the best time to do so. As shown in Figure 6.3, you can add a new blank page, add a page based on a template, or insert an existing document into the Web. To add a blank page, click the Add New Blank Page button, and the new page appears at the bottom of the list (you are given the option to rename pages in the next step of the wizard).

F I G U R E 6.3: Add Pages step of the Web Page wizard

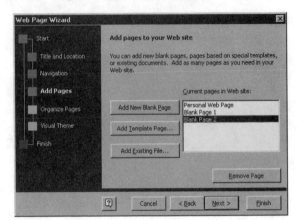

Using Templates

Word includes seven Web page templates. Some of these templates give you specific page layouts, such as the Left-Aligned Column and Right-Aligned Column templates. Others provide a structure for Web content, such as the Frequently Asked Questions and Table of Contents templates. To review each template, click the Add Template Page button in the Add Pages step. This opens the dialog box and preview window (see Figure 6.4). Click any of the templates in the Web Page Template dialog box to see a full-page view of the template. When you have chosen the template you want to include in your Web, click OK. If you'd like to add another template page, click Add Template Page again and repeat the process.

Adding Existing Documents

If you would like to convert any existing documents and add them to your Web, click the Add Existing File button in the Add Pages step. Locate and double-click a file you would like to include. The wizard saves a copy of the file as HTML and includes it in the Web folder. Repeat the process to add additional documents.

If you try to add an HTML page created in FrontPage 2000 or a page created in Excel or Access that uses the Office Web Components, it opens in its native application instead of being added in the wizard. When you have finished adding pages, click Next to move on to the Organize Pages step of the wizard.

F I G U R E 6.4: Previewing a Web page template

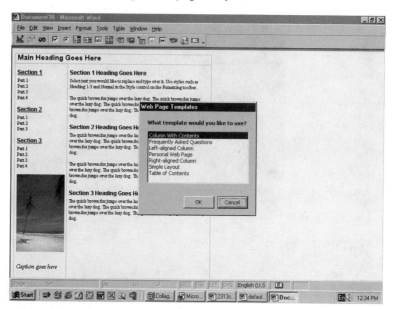

NOTE When you insert a file in the wizard, it is added as a single page, even if it's a multipage document. If you have a document that you want to include as several individual pages, use copy and paste to create and save a separate Word document for each page before launching the wizard, then insert each document.

Organizing the Links

Now that you have the pages in your Web, you can rename each page and change their relative order as shown in Figure 6.5. This order determines the order of the links. Use the Move Up and Move Down buttons to rearrange the pages and the Rename button to change a page's name. Click Next to move on to the next step.

F I G U R E   6.5: Putting the Web pages in order

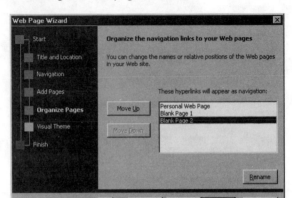

Applying Themes

A theme is a collection of colors, fonts, graphics, backgrounds, bullet characters, and styles that fit together. Office includes over 60 themes that can be applied to print publications, online documents, and Web pages. To select a theme, click the Browse Themes button in the Visual Theme step of the Web Page wizard.

The Theme dialog box, shown in Figure 6.6, displays a preview of each theme listed on the left. Options for Active Graphics (typically appearing as animated bullets and horizontal lines) and Background Image are on by default. If you would also like to use Vivid Colors, click the check box. You can see the results of turning these options on or off in the preview window on the right, although you won't see active graphics actually move.

Once you decide on a theme (you can also choose No Theme from the top of the list), click OK. If you decide to use a theme, make sure Add a Visual Theme is selected in the Visual Theme step of the wizard.

F I G U R E 6.6: Web themes

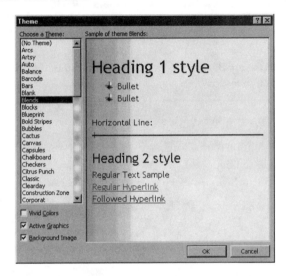

Click Next to move to the last step of the wizard, and then click Finish. The wizard creates your Web pages, adds the links you specified, and saves the pages to the folder you chose.

Creating a Web Using the Wizard

1. Click File ➤ New and choose the Web Pages tab of the New dialog box.

2. Select Web Page Wizard and click OK to begin.

3. Click Next to move past the Start step of the wizard to the Title and Location step. Enter a descriptive name and choose a file location for your Web.

4. At the Navigation step, choose a frame style.

5. Add blank pages, pages based on a template, or pages from existing files at the Add Pages step. Remove pages you don't want.

6. At the Organize Pages step, use the Move Up and Move Down buttons to put your pages in an order that makes sense. Rename pages if you wish by clicking the Rename button and typing the new name. When you're finished with this step. Click Next.

Creating a Web Using the Wizard *(continued)*

7. Browse to choose a visual theme for your page or choose the No Theme option.

8. Use the Back button to return to any step of the wizard and make changes, or Click Next and then Finish.

Exploring Web Files

In addition to the Web pages, the the Web Page wizard creates additional folders and files for your Web. To view these, open the folder in My Computer or Windows Explorer, as shown below.

You may notice a number of subfolders and files that you aren't familiar with. Default.htm is the filename the wizard automatically assigns to the first or home page of the Web (the home page of a Web that is published on a Web server is index.htm). The wizard creates a subfolder for each page and uses it to house graphics and other objects related to the page. For example, when you insert a graphic on a page and save the page, Word automatically saves the graphic to the page's corresponding subfolder. Graphics and other objects are not saved as part of a Web page but rather are saved separately and linked to the page. This is standard Web design protocol and helps keep the myriad of individual files streamlined and organized.

Viewing Your Web

After the Web Page wizard finishes its job, it opens the home page in Word. If you used frames in your Web site, the Frames toolbar opens (see more about frames in "Working with Frames" later in this chapter). The home page contains navigation links to other pages in the Web either in frames (as shown in Figure 6.7) or at the top the page if you choose the Separate Page option.

F I G U R E 6.7: Home page

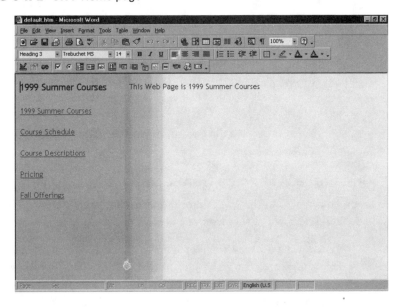

To view the other pages of the Web, point to any of the navigation links. The pointer changes to a hand and provides a ScreenTip about the file location of the hyperlink. Click the hyperlink to open the page. When the page opens, the Web toolbar, shown in Figure 6.8, also opens.

F I G U R E 6.8: The Web toolbar

The Web toolbar is the standard Internet Explorer browser toolbar. Click the Back button to return to the home page.

Hands On

1. Use the Web Page wizard to create a Web.

   a) Give your Web a descriptive name. If you don't want to use the default, browse to select a location for your Web.

   b) Use a vertical frame.

   c) Remove the Personal Web Page and add three new pages: one blank, one with a template, and one from an existing file.

   d) Organize the pages in an order that makes sense. Rename at least one page.

   e) Select a theme for your Web.

2. When you finish the wizard, browse the Web page by clicking the various links.

Creating a Web Page from Scratch

To begin a Word document for the Web from scratch, choose File ➤ New and select Web Pages from the New dialog box.

You now have access to all of Word's editing and formatting features to help you create your Web page. In addition, you can add themes by choosing Format ➤ Theme, hyperlinks by selecting text and choosing Edit ➤ Hyperlink, and frames by choosing Format ➤Frames. Frames and hyperlinks are covered in depth later in this chapter.

Adding Content to a Web Page

Editing Web pages in Word is not much different than editing other Word documents. You have access to all of Word's formatting and editing tools, including fonts, paragraph formatting, bullets, tables, borders, and shading. Although, overall, you will find Word's HTML tools to be consistent with the typical Word features you are used to using, there are some minor HTML restrictions.

Web pages also include features that are not typically used in print documents: hyperlinks, frames, form controls, active graphics such as scrolling text boxes, and other special multimedia features. If you learn to use these tools effectively, you'll be able to design Web pages that are dynamic, attractive, and effective.

Saving and Reopening a Web

Objective W2000.4.6

If you create a Web using the Web Page wizard, the wizard automatically saves the Web pages and associated files. After you make changes to any of the pages, click the Save button or choose File ➤ Save to resave the files just like you would any other document. When you start a Web page with a Web template, you can also save just as you would any other document.

Convert an existing document to a Web page by opening it and choosing File ➤ Save As Web Page. Select a location for your file, change its title if you wish, and click Save. If Word has to reformat existing objects, borders, shading, etc., you may be prompted to complete the conversion. After the document is saved as a Web page, you can reformat it, add a theme, and insert frames as desired.

When you reopen a Web, you can choose to open individual pages for editing or the entire Web. If you use frames, you can open separately each page displayed in the frames, or open the page that contains all the frame pages. To make changes to the structure of the frames page, open the file TOC Frame.htm (see more about working with frames later in this chapter). To open the home page, open the file called default.htm.

Saving a Web Page in Word

1. If you're converting a regular Word document to a Web page, choose File ➤ Save As Web Page.

2. Open the folder (or create a new folder) where you want to save your Web page.

3. Enter a title for the Web page, if desired.

4. Enter a filename and click Save.

5. If you created your Web using a wizard or template, Word automatically saves the pages in HTML format. Simply resave when you make changes by clicking the Save button on the Standard toolbar.

Round Tripping a Document from HTML (Heading Level 4)

Objective W2000E.7.6

In Word 2000, you can create, save, and edit HTML documents without having to convert them to Word's native format. When you save a Word document as a Web page, you can open the document in your Web browser just like any other Web document. You can also open this HTML document directly in Word for editing and updating. This process of saving a Web page in Word and then reopening it in Word for editing is called Round Tripping. Round Tripping makes it easy to make changes to a Web page posted on a corporate Web server without requiring users to learn another Web page editing tool.

Creating Hyperlinks

Objective W2000.4.8

Hyperlinks are what make the Web what it is. When Tim Berners-Lee, CERN researcher, developed HTML, his primary interest was in being able to access related documents easily, without regard to computer platform or operating system, by connecting the documents through a series of links. Hyperlinks allow readers to pursue their areas of interest without having to wade through tons of materials searching for specific topics. And hyperlinks take readers down paths they might never have traveled without the ease of clicking a mouse. Adding hyperlinks to your documents moves information down off the shelf, dusts it off, and makes it a living, breathing instrument that people can really use.

Creating a hyperlink in an existing Web page is easy. First you'll enter or select some descriptive text anywhere in the page to define the link; for example, you could type: `Click here to view new courses` or select the existing text that says `New Courses`. Then right-click the selected text, and choose Hyperlink to open the Insert Hyperlink dialog box, as shown in Figure 6.9. If you prefer, you can select the text and press Ctrl+K or choose Insert ➤ Hyperlink.

In the Insert Hyperlink dialog box, type a file or Web page name or click the File or Web Page button to browse for the file. Click the Place in This Document button to create a link to another location in the same document, or click the E-Mail Address button to create a link to an e-mail message form. If you want to change the hyperlink text, enter new text in the Text to Display box. Add a ScreenTip to the hyperlink by clicking the Screen-Tip button and entering the text you want to appear in a ScreenTip. Click OK to create the link.

NOTE For more about creating hyperlinks and bookmarks in Word documents, refer to Chapter 4.

F I G U R E 6.9: Insert Hyperlink dialog

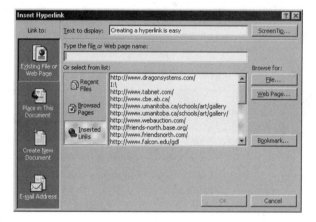

NOTE Word automatically creates a hyperlink when you type an address it recognizes as an Internet or file path address. If, for example, you type www.train2k.com, Word creates a hyperlink to that address. To turn hyperlink automatic formatting on or off, choose Tools ➢ AutoCorrect. Click AutoFormat As You Type and check or clear the Internet and Network Paths with Hyperlinks check box. Check or clear the same check box on the AutoFormat tab.

Creating a Hyperlink to a Web Page or File

1. Enter and select text that will serve as the hyperlink.

2. Right-click the selected text or Choose Insert ➢ Hyperlink to open the Insert Hyperlink dialog box.

Creating a Hyperlink to a Web Page or File *(continued)*

3. Choose a file, Web page, bookmark, or other existing document for the link by using the Insert Hyperlink dialog box options. After entering or selecting the filename and path, click OK to establish the link.

OR

4. To link to a page on the Web, enter the URL for the file. To locate the page, click the Browse for Web Page button, then click the Search the Web button to open the Link to File dialog box. Your default browser loads and opens a search engine at http://www.microsoft.com.

   Use the search engine, Favorites list, bookmarks, or another search engine to go to the Web page you wish to link to.

5. Switch back to Word.

6. Click OK to create the link.

Troubleshooting Hyperlinks

A hyperlink's effectiveness depends on its being able to locate the file or Internet address it is linked to. If the file has moved or been renamed, or the Web address no longer exists, clicking the hyperlink returns an error message. It's important to regularly verify hyperlinks you've included in your site. If a link does not work, check the following:

1. Do you currently have access to the Internet or intranet site the link is calling? If not, check the link again when access has been restored.

2. Has the site or file moved? If so, right-click the link and choose Edit ➤ Hyperlink. Update the location of the linked file.

3. Does the file still exist? If not, right-click the link and choose Edit ➤ Hyperlink. Click Remove Link.

If the link still does not work after you have followed these steps, make sure the address is spelled correctly and there are no syntax errors in the address (for example, a comma instead of a dot).

If Edit Hyperlink does not appear on the shortcut menu when you right-click, it could be because the text contains a spelling or grammar error. Word displays the Spelling shortcut menu until the error is corrected.

Inserting Graphics

Visitors to a Web site expect to see more than just text. Graphics add impact to your Web pages, as long as they are fast-loading. The trick is to use small, attention-grabbing graphics on main pages and give visitors the option to view larger, more elaborate graphics by clicking to another page.

Inserting a graphic into a Web page is no different than placing one in a Word document. The Clip Gallery is available from the Insert menu; from the gallery, you can choose art or any other clip art or photos you want to use (for more about inserting graphics, see Chapter 5).

Not all graphics features available in Word are supported by Web browsers. To ensure that your Web pages look as good being viewed by a browser as they do in Word, features that are unsupported have been disabled. Only some of the wrapping styles available in Word documents, for example, are available for use in Web pages. As a result, you may find that once you've inserted a graphic, you have difficulty positioning it where you want it. To change how text wraps around the picture so you can more easily place the graphic where you want it, right-click the graphic and choose Format Picture or choose Format ➤ Picture from the menu. Click the Layout tab and change the Wrapping Style, as shown in Figure 6.10.

F I G U R E 6.10: Changing wrapping style

A number of other options are available in the Format Picture dialog box. Because not all browsers can display graphics, and some people don't want to wait for graphics to appear on Web pages, it's possible to insert alternative text that describes the graphic. When the Web page opens, the alternative text appears while the page is loading, allowing visitors to click when they find the text they want without waiting for the graphic. To specify alternative text, click the Web tab of the Format Picture dialog box.

Troubleshooting Graphics

If you are having trouble positioning graphics on a Web page, you might want to try a Web designer's trick. Insert a table into the page. Three columns are usually sufficient, but add more columns if you want to line up a series of graphics. Then, position the graphic inside a cell of the table and change the table properties so the table expands to fill the screen.

1. Click inside the table and choose Table ➤ Table Properties.

2. Click the Table tab and changed Preferred Width to 100% Measured in Percent. (Although this step is not necessary, it makes it easier if you aren't sure about precise placement and sizing.) Click OK.

3. Now place the graphic inside the cell of the table that corresponds to the position you would like for the graphic. Click the Center button on the Formatting toolbar to center the graphic in the cell.

Before publishing the Web page, you can change the table's borders to No Borders. To do this, select the table, choose Format ➤ Borders and Shading, click the Borders tab, and click None. Your table won't be visible on the page, but the graphics stay where you put them.

Web Tools Toolbar

Word comes equipped with a Web Tools toolbar, shown in Figure 6.11, to help you add sounds and video, create forms, and add scrolling text. To turn on the Web Tools toolbar, choose View ➤ Toolbars and click Web Tools (not Web).

F I G U R E 6.11: The Web Tools toolbar

Adding Background Sounds and Movies

Despite the fact that we don't seem to mind being constantly barraged by sounds from radio and television, we have not yet developed a fondness for sounds from the Web. Only occasionally will you happen upon a Web site that opens with background music drawing you in (or turning you away). However, if you'd like to add background sounds to your site, Word makes it easy for you to do.

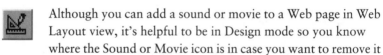

Although you can add a sound or movie to a Web page in Web Layout view, it's helpful to be in Design mode so you know where the Sound or Movie icon is in case you want to remove it later. Open the Web Tools toolbar, and click the Design Mode button to go into Design mode. Before inserting the Sound or Movie icon, move the insertion point to an obvious position at the top of the page. This is where the icon representing the sound or movie file will appear.

TIP You can move into Design mode from any view, not just Web Layout view, but if you're working on a Web page, it's best to begin in Web Layout view so you know what your finished product will look like.

When you're all set, click the Sound button on the Web Tools toolbar. Enter the name of a .wav file or click Browse and locate the file. Click the Loop down-arrow to choose the number of times you want the sound to play, either 1–5 or Infinite. Click OK. Click the Design Mode button to return to the view you were in when you clicked the Design Mode button. The sound file begins playing immediately and plays every time you open the page (and as many times as you instruct it to play).

TIP A user's browser (and add-ins like RealPlayer) determine the types of sound files they can play. MIDI and WAV files are common, but MP3 (MPEG audio) files are becoming the most common. After you insert the file, test it in your browser.

 To add a movie file, click the Movie button on the Web Tools toolbar (remember to click the Design Mode button and position the insertion point first). Enter the settings in the Movie Clip dialog box, as shown in Figure 6.12. It's a good idea to include an alternative image that will display in browsers not supporting movie clips, or put the clip on a page so users can choose whether or not to download it. However, even if a browser does support movie clips, the image will be small and difficult to see on most systems. If possible, test out the display on several machines with different browsers to see how the movie file looks before making it a permanent part of your Web page.

F I G U R E 6.12: Movie clip settings

Removing Sound or a Movie from a Web Page

 To remove a sound or movie clip, move into Design mode. Locate the Sound or Movie icon, as shown here. Select the icon and choose Edit ➢ Clear.

Adding Scrolling Text

Scrolling text is a way to grab your visitors' attention with a special announcement or notice. If you've used Windows Scrolling Marquee screen saver, you're already familiar with the concept. To add scrolling text, click the Design Mode button on the Web Tools toolbar, then position the insertion point where you want the scrolling text to appear.

 Click the Scrolling Text button on the Web Tools toolbar and enter the text in the text box, as shown in Figure 6.13. Set the options for Behavior, Direction, Background Color, Loop, and Speed and then click OK to insert the scrolling text box. If you want to view the scrolling text, click the Design Mode button to exit Design mode. Note, however, that the text box doesn't scroll in Design mode.

F I G U R E 6.13: Entering scrolling text

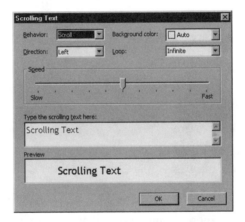

You can resize or move the scrolling text box in Design mode as you would any text box in Word. To delete a scrolling text box, switch to Design mode, click the box to select it, and press Delete.

Creating Web-Based Forms

To make the Web truly interactive, information has to go in both directions. Web users need the ability to send information to the site owners, and Web owners need to know about who their visitors are and what they are looking for. Web forms provide a way for visitors to respond to surveys, register with a site, voice their opinions about issues, search your site, or submit feedback.

You can add a form to any Web page. Word automatically adds Top of Form and Bottom of Form boundaries to the form, as shown in Figure 6.14, when you add a form control from the Web Tools toolbar.

F I G U R E 6.14: Form control navigators

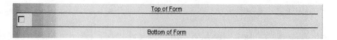

Word comes equipped with 11 built-in form controls for you to use on forms. These are:

- Check box control
- Option control
- Drop-down box control
- List box control
- Text box control
- Text area control
- Submit control
- Submit with image control
- Reset control
- Hidden control
- Password control

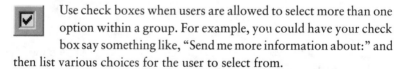 Use check boxes when users are allowed to select more than one option within a group. For example, you could have your check box say something like, "Send me more information about:" and then list various choices for the user to select from.

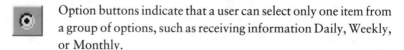 Option buttons indicate that a user can select only one item from a group of options, such as receiving information Daily, Weekly, or Monthly.

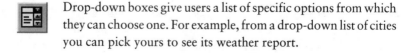 Drop-down boxes give users a list of specific options from which they can choose one. For example, from a drop-down list of cities you can pick yours to see its weather report.

List boxes are similar to drop-down boxes in that they give users a list of options to choose from. However, instead of clicking an arrow to open a list, users use scroll buttons to scroll through the list. List boxes allow users to select multiple choices by using Shift or Ctrl while clicking.

 Text boxes are fields where users can enter text, such as a name, address, or other specific information.

 Text areas are open text boxes with scroll bars where users can write a paragraph or more to give feedback, describe a problem, or provide other information.

 Submit buttons are essential elements on a form, because a user must click the Submit button so the data they entered is sent to the Web server for processing.

 The Submit with image control lets you substitute an image for the standard Submit button. Make sure users know they have to click this button to submit their data—and that clicking the button submits the data. For example, don't use the same image for a Next Page button and a Submit button.

 Reset is a form control that clears the data in the current form so the user can start over.

 Hidden is a form field, invisible to the user, that passes data to the Web server. For example, a hidden control could pass information about the user's operating system or Web browser.

 Password replaces typed text with asterisks so users can type passwords confidentially.

Laying Out a Form

Tables are a big help in laying out a form so it looks organized. Create the table so it has twice the number of columns you would want to display in a single row. For example, in Figure 6.15, the third row contains three fields, so the table contains six columns. After you have inserted all the field names and form controls, save the page and open it in Internet Explorer or another browser to see how it looks. (See "Previewing Web Pages" later in this chapter.)

FIGURE 6.15: Using a table to lay out form fields

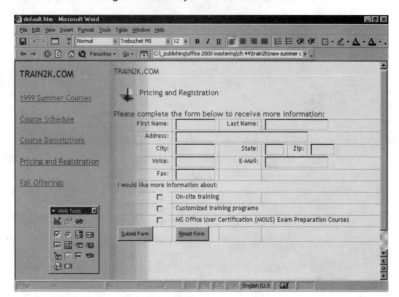

Setting Form Field Properties

All form controls have properties that determine how they behave. Some form controls require you to set the properties before the control can be used. For example, you must enter the values you want to appear in a drop-down box so the user has options to choose from. To set or edit a control's properties, double-click the control to open the Properties dialog box, as shown in Figure 6.16.

To enter options for a drop-down list or a list box, type the first value in the DisplayValues property. Enter a semicolon and no space before entering the next value. The values you type each appear on a separate line in the drop-down list or list box. To test the drop-down box, exit Design mode and click the down arrow on the form control.

It's helpful to any programmers who might work on your Web site if you change the name of a control from the default name to a name that describes the field, for example, change HTMLText1 to FirstName. Control names cannot contain spaces, but they can contain numbers and upper- and lowercase letters.

F I G U R E 6.16: Properties dialog box.

For more information about form control properties, refer to the Word Help file: *Form controls you can use on a Web page.*

NOTE Data submitted by Web forms is processed by the Web server and stored in a database format either as a comma-delimited text file, an Access table, or other database format. For a form to work, the Web server has to be set up to accept and process the data. Talk with your Web server administrator before publishing a form on a Web site.

Previewing Web Pages

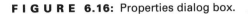

Objective W2000.3.3

The easiest and quickest way to see what your Web will look like in a browser window is to click File ➤ Web Page Preview. Your default browser launches, and the home page is displayed. Follow the links as you normally would and make notes if you see things you want to change. You can't edit in Web Page Preview, so when you're through previewing, close or minimize the browser window and return to Word to make necessary changes.

TIP If you're already in a browser window and want to preview your Web, click File ➤ Open. Locate the default.htm for the Web site you want to view. Click OK.

Using Web Page Preview

1. Click File ➤ Web Page Preview to open your default browser and view your Web.

2. Use navigation links to move from the home page of the Web site to the page on which you are working.

3. After you have viewed the page, close or minimize the browser and return to Word.

4. Make any additional changes you want to and save the Word Web page again.

5. Maximize the browser and click the Refresh button on the browser toolbar to view your changes.

NOTE Because of the way different browsers display form fields, it is difficult to make every field line up perfectly with the fields above it unless you use tables.

Working with Frames

A frame is a structure that displays a Web page on every other page of the Web site. The page that displays the frames is called a frames page. Although the Web Page wizard is the easiest way to create a simple navigational frame, Word offers you the option of adding and deleting frames manually if you prefer.

TIP Word has a Frames toolbar you can use to add, delete, and set the properties of frames. Right-click any toolbar and choose Frames to display the toolbar.

To add a frame, click Format ➤ Frames. If you only want to add a table of contents to the existing document, choose Table of Contents in Frame. This option creates a table of contents for the displayed document based on heading styles used in the document. Figure 6.17 shows an example of a Table of Contents frame. A link is created for each heading formatted using a heading style (for more about using heading styles, see Chapter 3).

F I G U R E 6.17: The Table of Contents in Frame option

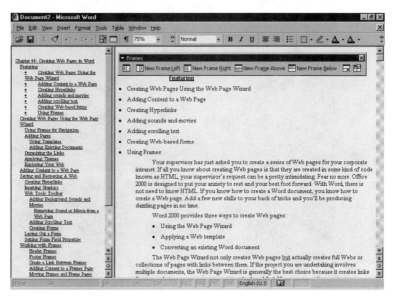

To create a frames page to which you can add frames, choose New Frames Page. Choose Format ➤ Frames again to choose the position of the frame you would like to add. You have several frame options, as shown below.

New Frame Above creates a header frame, and New Frame Below creates a footer frame. If you plan to add horizontal and vertical frames, add header and footer frames first so they extend the width of the page, as shown in Figure 6.18. Resize frames by dragging the frame border in the direction you want.

F I G U R E 6.18: Add header and footer horizontal frames

Add content to each frame. When you save the frames page, each page is saved separately as M, M1, M2, and so on.

Before saving a frames page, create a folder to save it in. Word automatically saves the frames as individual pages in that folder. If you add graphics or other objects, Word creates subfolders to house them. Give the frames page a name that reminds you it's a frames page. If it's the home page of the Web you are creating, save it as default.htm.

Setting Frame Properties

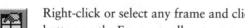 Right-click or select any frame and click the Frame Properties button on the Frames toolbar to open the Frame Properties dialog box, shown in Figure 6.19. The initial page should be set to the frame that is open. However, you can change the page that opens in a frames page by selecting a different initial page. Give the frame a name

by selecting or entering one in the Name box. Adjust the size of the frame by adjusting the size controls. By default, frames are set to a relative size. You can change the relative size to a specific pixel size or a percentage of the screen display by changing the Measure In option.

F I G U R E 6.19: Changing frame properties

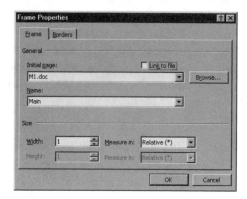

On the Borders tab of the Frame Properties dialog box, set whether or not you want to display frame borders and, if you do, what size and color you want them to be. You can determine if you want users to be able to adjust the frame size by clearing or checking the Frame Is Resizable in Browser check box. Turn scroll bars on or off using the Show Scrollbars in Browsers setting.

WARNING   If you move a frames page to a different folder or drive location, you must copy all of the related frames documents to the same location.

Removing a Frame from a Frames Page

If you decide you want to remove a frame from a frames page, click in the frame and choose Format ➢ Frames ➢ Delete Frame or click the Delete Frame button on the Frames toolbar. You may want to save the frame under a different name before you delete it in case you decide you want to use it at a later time. To save the frame under a different name, right-click in the frame and choose Save Current Frame As.

View HTML Source of a Web Page

Although Word 2000 provides some exciting Web page design options, creating a complex Web site requires some knowledge of HTML and other Web programming tools. While you are creating Web pages in Word, Word is writing the HTML code behind the scenes. You can view this code and even edit it directly by choosing View ➤ HTML Source. This opens the Microsoft Development Environment design window where you can edit HTML and active server page (.asp) files. If you are not a programmer, this is a good place to take a look at what it takes to produce the content you are creating and see HTML in actual application. If you are a programmer, you can edit the HTML file and add Microsoft Visual Basic, JScript, and VBScript to your files.

NOTE   The default installation of Word does not include the HTML viewer, so you may be prompted to install it.

Hands On

Objectives W2000.3.3 and 4.6

1. In a new or existing Web page:

   a) Select some text and add a hyperlink to another Web page. Add a hyperlink to an e-mail address.

   b) Test the hyperlinks.

   c) Open the Web and Web Tools toolbars. Switch to Design view and insert a sound clip that plays once when the page is opened.

   d) Create a simple Web form using two types of form controls. Edit the values using the Form Control Properties (right-click and choose Properties).

   e) Add a frame and modify its properties so the border is displayed.

   f) View the page in your browser using Web Page Preview.

   g) Save the changes you've made.

2. Open a Word document and use the Save As a Web Page command to convert it to HTML.

   a) Save the document in the same folder as the Web you created (or modified) in Step 1.

   b) Create a link to the new page from the Web you edited in Step 1.

CHAPTER

7

**Creating and Using
Macros in Office 2000**

Do you find yourself repeating the same Word task several times a day? If so, you'll be pleased to know there's a better way! Word macros offer hundreds of possibilities for placing shortcuts in your work, making you more efficient.

A *macro* is a set of instructions that a program executes on command. The instructions can be simple keystrokes or complex menu selections. If you have tasks you regularly complete that include the same series of steps, creating a macro to automate the task saves time and effort. If you're creating documents for others, adding a few macros can make the documents more user-friendly. In this chapter, you'll learn how to create and use macros to simplify your repetitive tasks in Word.

Recording a Simple Macro

Objective W2000E.6.2

Most macros complete repetitive tasks that involve several steps. You record (create) the series of steps you want to repeat. The next time you need to carry out the operation, you can run (play back) the macro to repeat the steps. Before recording a macro, you should practice the steps you want to record, because once you begin recording, all your actions are recorded—mistakes included. After you know the steps, determine what conditions your macro will operate under and set up those conditions. Will you always use the macro in a specific document? If so, open the document. Will the macro be used to change or format selected text or numbers? Then have the text or numbers selected before you begin recording the macro, just as you will when you play the macro back at a later time.

When you have practiced the steps and set up the same conditions under which the macro will run, select Tools ➤ Macro ➤ Record New Macro to open the Record Macro dialog box shown in Figure 7.1.

The suggested name is Macro1 (Microsoft didn't waste a lot of imagination here). Enter a more descriptive name for the macro, such as PrintFigures.

Macro names can be up to 255 characters long; they can contain numbers, letters, and underscores (but not spaces or other punctuation); and they must begin with a letter. Enter a new description. If other users will have access to the macro, include your name for reference.

F I G U R E 7.1: Record Macro dialog box

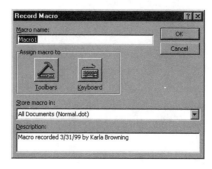

Storing a Macro

In the Store Macro In drop-down, select the document in which you want the macro stored. A macro's storage location determines how you'll be able to access it on playback.

- If you select the current document, then the macro will only be available in the current document. If you want the same macro somewhere else, you'll have to copy or re-create it. Macros that are stored in a document are *local macros*.

- Storing a macro in Normal.dot, the default template, creates a *global macro*, available to all documents created in the program.

From the description, you'd think you should save every macro as a global macro, but all the global macros will be loaded each time you launch Word. They'll take up space in memory, and any macro names you use here can't be reused in individual documents. Unless a macro is going to receive wide usage, it's best to store it in the current document.

Word lets you assign a shortcut or place the macro on the toolbar. While you can assign macros to shortcut keys, you should use extreme caution when making assignments. Most of the Ctrl+ combinations and many of the Ctrl+Shift combinations are already in use. It's safer to assign frequently used macros to a toolbar. You don't have to make this decision when you record the macro; you can always add a macro to a toolbar later (see "Customizing Toolbars" later in this chapter).

Once you've set the options in the dialog box, click the OK button to begin macro recording. The message "Recording" is displayed at the left end of the status bar to show you are recording a macro. The Stop Recording toolbar opens. The macro recorder records the actions you take, but not the delay between actions, so take your time. If you want the macro to enter text, enter the text now. Type carefully: If you make and correct a mistake, the mistake and correction will be included when you replay the macro until you edit the mistake (see "Editing Macros"). Make menu selections as you normally would to include them in the macro.

 When you are finished entering all the steps in the macro, click the Stop button on the Stop Recording toolbar. The toolbar will close automatically. You don't need to save the macro now. Local macros are saved when you save the document.

Word prompts you to save changes to Normal.dot when you end your Word session if the Prompt to Save Normal Template option (choose Tools ➤ Options ➤ Save) is enabled. If the option is not enabled, global macros are saved automatically.

Formatting Options in Macros

If you want to format text in a macro, choose the formatting options from a formatting dialog box rather than choosing the font, font style, size, and alignment by clicking toolbar buttons. If you use the buttons, the playback results will be unpredictable because the toolbar buttons are toggle buttons. If, for example, selected text is already italicized, clicking the Italics button will turn Italics off. Whenever possible, don't use format toggle buttons in macros unless you can guarantee that the text you select when you play back will be formatted exactly as the text was when you recorded the macro.

Opening a File with Macros

A *macro virus* is a computer virus written as a macro. When you open a document that contains a virus, the virus copies itself into the Normal template. From that point forward, every document you save using the Normal template will be infected, which means that every file you give to someone else on a disk or via the Internet will also contain the virus.

WARNING   Office 2000 does not include virus detection software. If you ever receive files from another computer by disk, network, or Internet connection, you should purchase quality virus protection software for your system.

Creating a Macro

1. Create the same conditions that will be in effect when you play the macro.

2. Choose Tools ➤ Record Macro ➤ Record New Macro to open the Record Macro dialog box.

3. Enter a Macro Name and Description.

4. Choose a storage location from the drop-down list.

5. Click OK to begin recording the macro.

6. Perform the steps you want included in the macro.

7. Click the Stop button on the Stop Recording toolbar when you have finished recording the steps of the macro.

Macro Protection

Word 2000 offers three levels of macro protection: low, medium, and high. Choose which level you prefer to maintain by clicking Tools ➤ Macro ➤ Security.

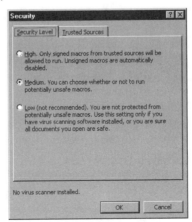

High security allows you to enter a list of trusted sources and Word won't open a document that contains macros signed by anyone not on the list of trusted sources. If you choose Medium, Word notifies you if any macros exist in a document you are trying to open. You can decide whether you want to open the document with macros enabled or to disable them. Disabling the macros gives you an opportunity to look at them in the Visual Basic Editor without endangering your computer. If you later decide you want to enable the macros, just close and then reopen the file.

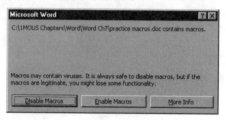

If you know the document contains macros you or a co-worker put there, choose Enable Macros. If, on the other hand, you received the workbook, unsolicited, from someone whose Internet name is HackU, you should consider disabling the macros or not opening the file.

Choosing low security effectively disables Word's macro detection feature. It's not a good idea to use low security unless you scan all documents with another virus checking program prior to opening them.

Updating Macros from Previous Versions

Some earlier versions of Word used a macro programming language called Word Basic. When you open a Word document from a prior version that contains macros, Word 2000 automatically converts the macros.

Running Macros

It's always a good idea to save anything you have open before you run a new macro. If you make a mistake during recording, the playback results may not be what you expected. (If there was an error, you can record the macro again using the same name. You might also have to click Undo a few times to back out of any problems the macro created.) To run a macro, choose Tools ➤ Macro ➤ Macros to open the Macros dialog box, shown in Figure 7.2. Select the macro from the list below the Macro Name control, and then click the Run button. The macro will execute one step at a time.

You can't enter text or choose menu options while the macro is executing. When the macro is done playing, the application will return control to you.

F I G U R E 7.2: Macros dialog box

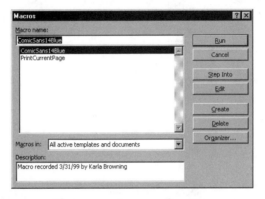

Running a Macro

1. Choose Tools ➢ Macro ➢ Macros.

2. Select the macro from list of available macros and click Run.

Examining and Editing Macros

Word 2000 macros are stored in Visual Basic *modules* and edited in the Visual Basic Editor. To examine or edit a macro, choose Tools ➢ Macro ➢ Macros to open the Macros dialog box, select the macro you want to examine, and then click the Edit button to open the Visual Basic Editor, shown in Figure 7.3.

The Visual Basic window may contain a number of windows. In Figure 7.3, a Properties window is open on the left and a Code window on the right. You can scroll through the Visual Basic Code window to see the information recorded in a macro. The macro name and description appear at the top of the macro. Programming code follows, beginning with the word Sub. If you know VBA programming language, you can create macros and other procedures directly by typing Visual Basic code into a module's Code window. If you want to learn about Visual Basic, recording macros and studying the resulting code is a good way to begin. Even if you don't understand Visual Basic, you can do some simple editing here.

F I G U R E 7.3: Visual Basic Editor

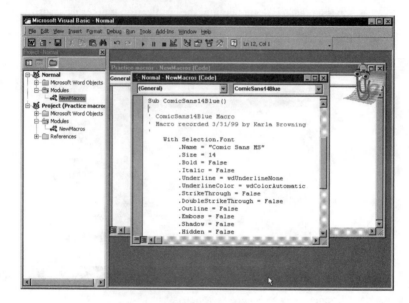

Using the example shown in Figure 7.3, you could easily change the font size from 14 to 12 by editing the number on the "size" line of code.

Editing a Macro

1. Choose Tools ➢ Macro ➢ Macros to open the Macros dialog box.

2. Select the macro and click the Edit button.

3. Make the changes you desire.

4. Save the macro and close the Visual Basic window.

Adding Macros to a Toolbar

Objective W2000E.6.7

To add an existing macro to a toolbar, right-click any toolbar and choose Customize or choose View ➢ Toolbars ➢ Customize to open the Customize dialog box. Click the Commands tab to open the Commands page, shown in Figure 7.4.

F I G U R E 7.4: Commands tab of the Customize dialog box

Select Macros from the Categories list on the left.

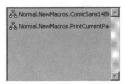

To add a menu item, drag the macro from the Commands list to the menu bar. If you want to place the custom menu item on an existing drop-down menu, move to the menu, hover a moment, and the menu will open. Drop the menu item where you want it to appear on the menu.

To add a toolbar button, drag the macro and drop it on the appropriate toolbar. If you drop it on an existing button, the other buttons will move over to make room for the new button. (Be careful here—buttons will move to the right, so you can't see them on the screen unless you scroll the toolbar.)

While the Customize dialog box is open, you can modify all the command bars. Drag menu items or buttons to new locations to rearrange them, or drop them in the document window to delete them. To add something other than a macro, scroll the Categories and Commands lists until you find the command you want. Drag the command onto a menu or toolbar. If you mess things up completely, you can always select and reset the menu bar and the toolbars on the Toolbars page of the Customize dialog box.

This is a great opportunity to add the toolbar buttons you've always wanted. To create an entirely new toolbar, click the New button on the Toolbars page. Drag any buttons you wish onto the toolbar from the Commands list. To copy a button from an existing toolbar, click the check box in front of the toolbar to activate it and then hold Ctrl while dragging the button (if you don't hold Ctrl, you'll move the button off the original toolbar).

Changing Command Item Settings

After you've placed your button or menu item, leave the Customize dialog box open and right-click the item you just placed to open the shortcut menu.

The button or menu item is attached to the macro you dragged to the command bar and the description defaults to whatever you named the macro. Choose Change Button Image from the shortcut menu to open a menu of icons you can assign to a command item. If you prefer, you can label the button or menu item by changing the contents of the Name box on the shortcut menu. The ampersand (&) is used on menu items and appears before the letter that a user can press to choose the menu item. The letter will be underlined on the menu bar like the F in File and E in Edit.

You can also create your own button images. While you are still in the Customize mode, select the button, right-click to get the shortcut menu, and then choose Edit Button Image to open the Button Editor to edit the button image.

When you are finished adding menu items, assigning macros, and sprucing up your button images, close the Customize dialog box. Now you can play the macro by clicking a toolbar button or making a menu selection. To remove a button or menu item, reopen the Customize dialog box and drag the item off the menu or toolbar.

Adding a Macro to a Menu or Toolbar

1. If the macro is not global, open the document that contains the macro.

2. Right-click any toolbar and choose Customize. Click the Commands tab.

3. Choose Macros from the Categories list.

4. Drag the macro onto a toolbar or menu.

5. Edit the button or menu name and/or image by right-clicking the item and choosing from the shortcut menu.

6. Click Close in the Customize dialog box when you're finished.

Copying, Deleting, and Renaming Macros

▶ *Objective W2000E.6.3*

Deleting Macros

Deleting a macro is easy. Renaming and copying macros is a bit more complex. To delete a macro, open the Macros dialog box, select the macro, and then click the Delete button. If you have recorded a macro and are not pleased with the way it executes, you can record the macro again using the same name. You will be asked if you want to overwrite (delete) the existing macro.

Copying and Renaming Macro Project Items

A major benefit of Office 2000 is that you can use Visual Basic to control the applications. You can create Word macros using the Macro Recorder or by typing Visual Basic code in the Visual Basic Editor. While you may prefer to create all your macros with the Recorder, if you need to copy, edit, or rename macros, you'll need to understand how macros are stored in Office 2000, and spend some time getting cozy with the Organizer and the Visual Basic Integrated Development Environment (IDE).

Macros are kept in *modules* stored with a Word document or template. A document can have more than one module, but Word creates a default module named NewMacros for local macros that you create. (Global macros are stored in modules attached to `Normal.dot`.) Modules, forms, and other Visual Basic objects are all macro project items. Rename or copy a Word macro project item in the Organizer. The Organizer dialog box is a central point for copying styles, AutoText, toolbars, and macro projects. Open two documents or templates in the Organizer, and then copy macro projects from one to the other. To access the Organizer dialog box, shown in Figure 7.5, choose Tools ➤ Templates and Add-Ins and click Organizer or Choose Tools ➤ Macro ➤ Macros and click the Organizer button. Click the Macro Project Items tab. Use the Macro Project Items Available In drop-down lists to select two open documents or templates. If the document or template you want to work with is not open, click one of the Close File buttons. An Open File button will appear so you can open the file. Select the macro project item you want to copy, then click the Copy button to copy it to the other document or template. To remove a macro project item from a document, select the macro project and click Delete. Click Rename to rename the selected macro item.

F I G U R E   7.5:   In the Organizer dialog box, you can delete, copy, and rename macros.

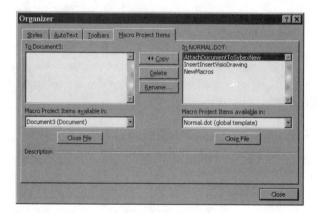

Renaming, Copying, and Moving Macros

To rename, copy, or move an individual macro, you have to use the Visual Basic Editor, part of the VB IDE, to open the macro project item or document that contains the macro. To fire up the Editor, choose Tools ➤ Macro ➤ Visual Basic Editor. If you want to work with a particular macro, it's faster to choose Tools ➤ Macro ➤ Macros, select the macro in the Macros dialog box, and then click the Edit button. When the VB Editor opens, the macro you want to work with will be open, as shown in Figure 7.6.

F I G U R E 7.6: Rename, copy, move, and delete macros in the VB Editor.

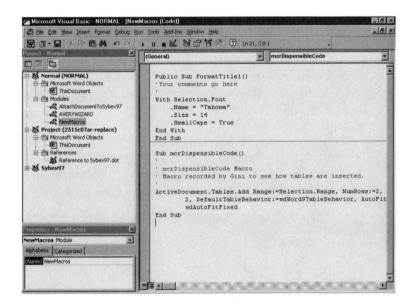

The Project Explorer is displayed on the left side of the VB window. The Explorer shows every open project: the document and accompanying Visual Basic objects (which were referred to in Word as macro project items) included with the document. If you double-click an object in the Project Explorer, it opens in the Visual Basic Editor.

The Editor is the large window on the right side of the window. Macros are VB subroutines, so each macro begins with the word Sub followed by the name of the macro, and ends with the command End Sub. To copy a macro, select all the text from the opening Sub to the closing End Sub, then use one of the copy/paste techniques you'd use in Word. Use cut and paste to move a macro from one macro project item to another.

TIP You can paste a macro in another document or module by opening the module or document in the Project Explorer, then pasting your macro code in the Editor window.

To rename a macro, select the macro name (following the opening Sub) and type a new name. If you're interested in learning about Visual Basic's use in Office 2000, spend some time in the VB IDE. Create a couple of macros, then open them in the Editor and see what makes them tick. When you're finished browsing, renaming, and copying macros, choose File ➤ Close and Return to Microsoft Word to save your changes and close the VB IDE.

When you have mastered the information in this chapter and want to learn more, choose Help ➤ Microsoft Word Help from the menu bar and enter macros in the dialog box to find more information.

Hands On

Objectives W2000E.6.2, E.6.3, and E.6.7

1. Open a new or existing document in Word. Record a global macro that checks the spelling in the active document and sends the document to the printer. Name the macro SpellPrint. Add it to the Standard toolbar and test it.

2. In the same document, record a global macro that

   a) Opens the Page Setup dialog box.

   b) Inserts a header with your name and the current date.

   c) Sets all four margins at 1 inch.

d) Changes the paper orientation to Landscape.

Name the macro `StandardPageSetup`. Execute the macro to see that it works the way you designed it.

3. Edit the above macro so the Paper Orientation is set to Portrait.

4. Create a local macro that turns table gridlines off.

   a) Add the macro to a toolbar button.

   b) Delete the macro and toolbar button.

5. Rename the macros you created.

6. Use the Organizer to copy the macro project from Exercise 3 or 4 to a blank document.

   a) Open the Macros dialog box to verify that the macro was copied.

   b) Open the macro in the VB Editor; rename the macro. Run the macro using its new name.

   c) Open the VB Editor and delete the macro from the new document.

APPENDIX

A

**Preparing for the Microsoft
Office 2000 User Specialist Exams**

A Microsoft Office User Specialist (MOUS) is a person who has passed an exam administered through a Microsoft Authorized Testing Center on one of the Office 2000 products. The exam was first introduced in 1997 as the Microsoft Certified Office User Program. Today users can receive designation as Microsoft Office User Specialists at the core level in Word, Excel, PowerPoint, Access, and Outlook (FrontPage and PhotoDraw core exams should be available soon). For those who really want to demonstrate their skills, exams are also available at Expert and Master levels.

Although the Office certification process is relatively new, Microsoft is experienced at certification. It currently offers several highly respected certification programs such as the Microsoft Certified System Engineer program and the Microsoft Certified Professional program. Up until now, all of these certifications focused on networking, systems, or programming skills. They were not intended for end users, but rather they were designed to establish recognizable standards for computer professionals—those people whose lifework revolves around computer systems.

The MOUS Difference

The Microsoft Office User Specialist certification is fundamentally different from other certifications that Microsoft offers. Whether it is in a large corporation or a small office, a MOUS is likely employed in a profession outside of the computer field, using applications such as Word and Excel to function effectively as an administrative assistant, a manager, an account representative, or a myriad other positions that require day-to-day problem-solving skills. The Microsoft Office family of products has helped this person accomplish the impossible to meet deadlines, impress supervisors or clients, and perform a job more efficiently. The MOUS is interested in improving skills and increasing opportunities. As more and more employers begin looking for verification of a person's software skills, there is no better way to stand out than to show your credentials as a specialist in the software the job requires.

> **NOTE** Although the MOUS program got off to a slow start, over 900 testing centers around the world have now delivered well over 30,000 exams.

Should I Become a Microsoft Office User Specialist?

If you were applying for an office job only a few short years ago, probably the only test you had to take was a typing test. This test would document your speed and accuracy at a typewriter. It didn't matter if you understood what you typed or if you could create a similar document from scratch—all you had to be able to do was recreate what someone handed to you and do it in an acceptable amount of time. With the infiltration of computers into large and small workplaces everywhere, the expectations placed on office workers have increased significantly.

Typing speed and accuracy may still be important, but even more valuable is knowledge about how to make the most efficient and effective use of new office technology. Microsoft Office 2000 is the fastest growing office suite on the market today. Knowing how to apply this group of powerful applications to the demands of your work environment can clearly put you ahead of the pack. You immediately stand out from the typists and become recognized as a problem-solver (and in some cases, even a life-saver to those who may be in a position to help advance your career).

If you are in business for yourself, you may not care about whether you can prove your skills to someone else, but being able to influence potential clients with the quality of your written and verbal presentations may make the difference between your business's success and failure. With little validation available from co-workers, the small-business person has to find other ways to feel confident in their skills, to know they are effectively using state-of-the-art technology to impress their clients.

The Microsoft Office User Specialist program provides a mechanism for all types of users, regardless of their motivation, to prove their competency in the family of Microsoft Office 2000 applications. Whether you are a student with little real-world experience or a highly trained professional with a top-level staff position, you may find it is beneficial to add the Microsoft Office User Specialist designation to your portfolio.

Getting an Employer to Foot the Bill

Companies that place a high value on employee education and training may very well agree to pay for an employee to take one or more of the MOUS exams. As the credential is becoming widely known, more and more employers are looking at the MOUS credential as a mark of excellence in their company. Certainly, there is no hard and fast rule about this—employers are by no means required to pay for them. However, it certainly doesn't hurt to ask a supervisor or Human Resource Department. Some companies may agree to reimburse an employee only if the exam is passed—it doesn't pay for them to spend money for someone to fail it.

Unless a company has issued a statement about paying for the exams, do your homework before approaching an employer. It helps if a company plans to adopt or has already adopted Office 2000 as the company standard. Visit the Microsoft Office User Certification Web site at http://www.mous.net, as well as other Office certifications sites, such as http://www.officecert.com offered by Quick Start Technologies, for more information (ammunition) to convince an employer of the benefits of employing certified employees.

If you decide to give an employer the opportunity to demonstrate a commitment to quality improvement and staff development, here are a few tips for you to consider when you are preparing a proposal to give to your supervisor:

- Plan to study for the exams on your own time. If you spend an hour after work or at lunch three or four times a week working through this book, you'll be ready to take one or even two of the exams after just a few study sessions. By doing it on your own time, it shows that you can take initiative and that you are committed to personal improvement. Even if this doesn't impress an employer, you will have improved your skills to help you in other areas of your job (or to get a better job!).

- Become familiar with Microsoft's requirements and the process for taking the exams so you are prepared to answer any question an employer may ask about how the exams work.

- List at least three specific benefits to a company for having certified employees. Be able to point out the financial savings resulting from fewer technical support calls and from less time wasted trying to solve dilemmas.

- Develop an argument that ties your getting certified into the company's overall quality initiative. Having certified employees in every field helps a company demonstrate to their customers and potential customers that they are committed to quality. It makes the company look good, and that goes a long way in today's competitive market.

- Offer to be a mentor to other employees—individually or as a group. If work time is too precious, organize a weekly bag lunch for Office users; ask a different person to present a different topic each week based on a project they just completed. However you approach it, show your employer you are a leader and it may be easier to make a case for the value of the certifications to the company.

If all else fails, pay for the exams yourself. Being certified makes you a more valuable commodity and may make your employer think twice when he or she sees you using Word to update your resume!

What are the Microsoft Office 2000 User Specialist Designations?

Once you've decided to pursue certification, you have to determine whether you want to take all the exams or pick and choose among them. Unless you plan to train other users or you have a technical support type job, you probably don't have a need to take all of the exams available. However, if you want a comprehensive knowledge base and you want the new plum of Office Specialist that Microsoft has placed on the platter, you may want to set up a plan of attack and go after them all.

It's possible to receive designation as a Specialist in each of six applications that are a part of the Microsoft Office family. These include Word, Excel, PowerPoint, Access, and Outlook. Because Word and Excel are the most popular of the six products and have the most widespread application, two levels of designation—Core and Expert—have been developed for these applications; that means there is a separate test for each level.

Microsoft expects that a Microsoft Office User Specialist at the Core level is able to complete the everyday tasks that arise in a typical office setting. A Word Specialist should be able to format text and paragraphs, create tables and columns, manage files, and work with pictures and charts. An Excel Specialist should be able to format cells and worksheets, enter formulas and basic functions, work with multiple worksheets, create charts, and insert objects.

In order to become an Expert Specialist, you are expected to be able to create more complex documents. A Word Expert should be able to conduct mail merges to create personalized form letters with envelopes and mailing labels, work with master and subdocuments, add references and use collaboration features. An Excel Expert should be able to use templates, work with multiple workbooks, create macros, use analysis tools, and use collaboration features.

The eight Specialist designations currently available are:

- Microsoft Office User Specialist: Microsoft Word 2000
- Microsoft Office User Specialist: Microsoft Word 2000 Expert
- Microsoft Office User Specialist: Microsoft Excel 2000
- Microsoft Office User Specialist: Microsoft Excel 2000 Expert
- Microsoft Office User Specialist: Microsoft PowerPoint 2000
- Microsoft Office User Specialist: Microsoft Outlook 2000
- Microsoft Office User Specialist: Microsoft Access 2000
- Microsoft Office User Specialist: Microsoft Office 2000 Master

To Be Developed

The MOUS program is still relatively new. Administration of the program was only taken over by Nivo International in late 1998. As a result, not all the anticipated exams have been developed as of this book's publication date.

Exam objectives, however, have been released for the following anticipated designations:

- Microsoft Office User Specialist: Microsoft PowerPoint 2000 Expert
- Microsoft Office User Specialist: Microsoft Access 2000 Expert

- Microsoft Office User Specialist: Microsoft Outlook 2000 Expert
- Microsoft Office User Specialist: Microsoft FrontPage 2000
- Microsoft Office User Specialist: Microsoft FrontPage 2000 Expert
- Microsoft Office User Specialist: Microsoft PhotoDraw 2000
- Microsoft Office User Specialist: Microsoft PhotoDraw 2000 Expert

Check `www.mous.net` for updates on the availability of these additional exams.

What Are the Exams Like?

Taking an exam is a lot like completing the Hands On exercises in each chapter of this book. You will be expected to apply your knowledge of an application to real-world tasks that you will complete within the application itself. Unlike other Microsoft certification exams, there are no multiple-choice questions. Instead, each user is expected to complete specific tasks, such as formatting a document in a certain way, creating a formula, sorting a list, etc. The exams must be completed within the designated time-frame, which is under an hour depending on the exam.

This is not a paper-and-pencil test. You will be working with a fully functional, live version of the product on which you are being tested. You can use all features of the product, including Help. However, if you access Help too often, you'll run out of time before completing all the required tasks.

When you're ready to start, take a deep breath (be sure to exhale too!) and click the Start Test button. Complete each task on the sample documents provided to you so you don't have to spend time creating documents of your own. Each task has a set of instructions for you to follow. When you've completed one task, click Next Task.

WARNING   Be aware: there is no going back to a previous task. Once you've move passed a particular task, it's gone forever.

Preparing to Take an Exam

Before you start studying, review the objectives for the test you are interested in taking. If you're an experienced user, you may even want to check off those activities in which you are already pretty comfortable. Spend some time reviewing those activities and making sure you are 100% confident in completing each of them. When you are ready to tackle new ground, either follow in order the topics of this book, or use the certification map to jump to the activities on which you want to focus.

If you are a relatively new user, you will benefit most from following in order each topic in this book, completing the Hands On exercises and then moving on to the next topic. When you have completed the book, review the objectives again and make sure you can complete each activity comfortably. If you need to review a topic for a second time, refer to the certification map at the end of this chapter to find out where it is covered in the book.

If you'd like to get a taste of how the exams work, download the practice exams from the www.mous.net site. You'll find practice exams for Word, Excel, and PowerPoint. They help you get used to the format and the structure of the exams so you'll know what to expect when you sit down to take the real ones.

Registering to Take an Exam

You can receive information about a local Authorized Testing Center (ACT) by calling 800-933-4493 or visiting the Web site of the company that manages the testing, Nivo International, at http://www.mous.net. Not every city has a testing center, but the number of centers is growing rapidly—there is probably a center within a couple hours' drive of you, if not right in your city. Although some centers allow walk-in test-takers, it's best to call first to make sure.

Each test you take has a fee associated with it. You can usually pay by check or credit card—check out payment arrangements when you call to register. Be sure to bring a picture ID (driver's license, passport, credit card, etc.) to the testing center with you.

Taking More than One Exam

It's not unusual that you may want to take more than one exam in a day, especially if the testing center is a distance from your house. Be careful not to overload yourself, however. Some people may be able to handle taking three or four in a day; others may faint after taking one. Evaluate how long you can realistically concentrate without affecting your ability to think clearly. There's no point in paying for an exam and then not allowing yourself optimal test taking conditions.

If you plan to take more than one exam, talk with the testing center about spacing them out a bit throughout the day. Take one or two then go to lunch before taking another one or two. You'll be fresher and have time enough to refocus on the new topic (maybe even get in a little last-minute cramming).

Getting Help When You're Stuck

You can't bring notes, books, or a laptop computer into the testing center; however, you can use the application's Help files for a quick refresher during the test. If you are concerned that you might have to look something up during the exam, practice using Help extensively before going in. You may find yourself failing the exam because you wasted valuable seconds searching through Help files. Find the most efficient ways to locate the steps you need to accomplish a task. Use the Index to search for what you need.

If you know there are a couple of areas you are weak on, look up the topics in the Index ahead of time so you'll know what you are looking for and when you have found it. Stay away from using the Office Assistant while you are taking an exam. Even though they may be cute, they take up precious time just appearing and disappearing. Save them for when you have the time to be entertained!

The Moment of Truth

The tests are scored electronically, and you'll find out your score immediately. You need to get about 80% correct to pass the tests. If you pass, you'll receive a certificate of completion in the mail in one or two weeks after taking the test. Take yourself out to dinner to celebrate, or better yet, have someone else take you out!

What Happens If I Don't Pass?

If you need to take a test again, ask the test administrator for a printed score report, which identifies where you need to focus your energy as you prepare for another round. You'll be told what areas you need to focus on. If you realize that you didn't know how to do certain tasks that were asked for, study up on those and then be sure to review all the material before taking the test again. Of course, you'll have to pay to take a test again, but it was probably money well spent. You learned some things and, although it would be nice to not be out the exam fee, being more experienced means you'll probably pass next time.

If you thought you were prepared but still didn't pass, you may have had test anxiety that probably won't be as bad the second time around; you'll be in familiar surroundings and know what is expected of you.

The Certification Map

The tables on the pages that follow list the skill sets and activities required for the Microsoft Office User Specialist: Microsoft Word 2000 Core and Word 2000 Expert exams. Also listed are the page numbers in this book where you'll find information about each of the activities.

T A B L E A.1: Word 2000 Core Activities

Standardized Coding Number	Activities	Page Numbers
W2000.1	**Working with text**	
W2000.1.1	Use the Undo, Redo, and Repeat command	14, 19, 41
W2000.1.2	Apply font formats (Bold, Italic, and Underline)	41, 47
W2000.1.3	Use the Spelling feature	32, 38
W2000.1.4	Use the Thesaurus feature	37, 38
W2000.1.5	Use the Grammar feature	34, 38
W2000.1.6	Insert page breaks	72, 81
W2000.1.7	Highlight text in document	45, 47
W2000.1.8	Insert and move text	12, 13
W2000.1.9	Cut, Copy, Paste, and Paste Special using the Office clipboard	16, 19
W2000.1.10	Copy formats using the Format Painter	46, 47

T A B L E A.1: Word 2000 Core Activities *(continued)*

Standardized Coding Number	Activities	Page Numbers
W2000.1.11	Select and change font and font size	41, 47
W2000.1.12	Find and replace text	69, 81
W2000.1.13	Apply character effects (superscript, subscript, strikethrough, small caps, and outline)	43, 47
W2000.1.14	Insert date and time	54, 55
W2000.1.15	Insert symbols	53, 55
W2000.1.16	Create and apply frequently used text with AutoCorrect	38, 67
W2000.2	**Working with paragraphs**	
W2000.2.1	Align text in paragraphs (Center, Left, Right, and Justified)	56, 66
W2000.2.2	Add bullets and numbering	48, 55
W2000.2.3	Set character, line, and paragraph spacing options	44, 47, 60, 66
W2000.2.4	Apply borders and shading to paragraphs	109
W2000.2.5	Use indentation options (Left, Right, First Line, and Hanging Indent)	57, 66
W2000.2.6	Use Tabs command (Center, Decimal, Left, and Right)	62, 66
W2000.2.7	Create an outline style numbered list	122, 123
W2000.2.8	Set tabs with leaders	64
W2000.3	**Working with documents**	
W2000.3.1	Print a document	25, 27, 77, 81

T A B L E A.1: Word 2000 Core Activities *(continued)*

Standardized Coding Number	Activities	Page Numbers
W2000.3.2	Use Print Preview	25, 27, 75, 81
W2000.3.3	Use Web Page Preview	249, 254
W2000.3.4	Navigate through a document	8, 13
W2000.3.5	Insert page numbers	85, 91
W2000.3.6	Set page orientation	72, 81
W2000.3.7	Set margins	74, 81
W2000.3.8	Use GoTo to locate specific elements in a document	8
W2000.3.9	Create and modify page numbers	85, 91
W2000.3.10	Create and modify headers and footers	87, 91
W2000.3.11	Align text vertically	73
W2000.3.12	Create and use newspaper columns	92, 95
W2000.3.13	Revise column structure	93, 95
W2000.3.14	Prepare and print envelopes and labels	78, 81
W2000.3.15	Apply styles	113, 116
W2000.3.16	Create sections with formatting that differs from other sections	72, 81, 84, 91
W2000.3.17	Use Click and Type	10, 13
W2000.4	**Managing files**	
W2000.4.1	Use Save	21, 24
W2000.4.2	Locate and open an existing document	23, 24

T A B L E A.1: Word 2000 Core Activities *(continued)*

Standardized Coding Number	Activities	Page Numbers
W2000.4.3	Use Save As (different name, location, or format)	22, 24
W2000.4.4	Create a folder	22, 24
W2000.4.5	Create a new document using a wizard	126, 127
W2000.4.6	Save as Web page	237, 254
W2000.4.7	Use templates to create a new document	123, 127
W2000.4.8	Create hyperlinks	169, 238
W2000.4.9	Use the Office Assistant	30, 32
W2000.4.10	Send a Word document via e-mail	191
W2000.5	**Using tables**	
W2000.5.1	Create and format tables	96, 111
W2000.5.2	Add borders and shading to tables	108, 111
W2000.5.3	Revise tables (insert and delete rows and columns, change cell formats)	102, 111
W2000.5.4	Modify table structure (merge cells, change height and width)	103, 105, 111
W2000.5.5	Rotate text in a table	101, 111
W2000.6	**Working with pictures and charts**	
W2000.6.1	Use the Drawing toolbar	209, 222
W2000.6.2	Insert graphics into a document (WordArt, clip art, images)	201, 208, 222

TABLE A.2: Word 2000 Expert Activities

Standardized Coding Number	Activity	Page Numbers
W2000E.1	**Working with paragraphs**	
W2000E.1.1	Apply paragraph and section shading	109
W2000E.1.2	Use text flow options (Widows/Orphans options and keeping lines together)	90, 91
W2000E.1.3	Sort lists, paragraphs, tables	137, 139
W2000E.2	**Working with documents**	
W2000E.2.1	Create and modify page borders	109
W2000E.2.2	Format first page differently than subsequent pages	86, 91
W2000E.2.3	Use bookmarks	167, 176
W2000E.2.4	Create and edit styles	114, 116
W2000E.2.5	Create watermarks	215
W2000E.2.6	Use find and replace with formats, special characters and nonprinting elements	70
W2000E.2.7	Balance column length (using column breaks appropriately)	92, 95
W2000E.2.8	Create or revise footnotes and endnotes	164, 176
W2000E.2.9	Work with master documents and subdocuments	178, 191
W2000E.2.10	Create and modify a table of contents	174, 176
W2000E.2.11	Create cross-references	169, 176
W2000E.2.12	Create and modify an index	171, 176

T A B L E A.2: Word 2000 Expert Activities *(continued)*

Standardized Coding Number	Activity	Page Numbers
W2000E.3	**Using tables**	
W2000E.3.1	Embed worksheets in a table	194, 200
W2000E.3.2	Perform calculations in a table	110
W2000E.3.3	Link Excel data as a table	195, 200
W2000E.3.4	Modify worksheets in a table	197, 200
W2000E.4	**Working with pictures and charts**	
W2000E.4.1	Add bitmapped graphics	205, 208
W2000E.4.2	Delete and position graphics	204, 208
W2000E.4.3	Create and modify charts	217, 222
W2000E.4.4	Import data into charts	218, 222
W2000E.5	**Using mail merge**	
W2000E.5.1	Create main document	140, 153
W2000E.5.2	Create data source	131, 139
W2000E.5.3	Sort records to be merged	137, 139, 147
W2000E.5.4	Merge main document and data source	143, 153
W2000E.5.5	Generate labels	149, 153
W2000E.5.6	Merge a document using alternate data sources	144, 153
W2000E.6	**Using advanced features**	
W2000E.6.1	Insert a field	158, 163
W2000E.6.2	Create, apply, and edit macros	258, 270

TABLE A.2: Word 2000 Expert Activities *(continued)*

Standardized Coding Number	Activity	Page Numbers
W2000E.6.3	Copy, rename, and delete macros	267, 270
W2000E.6.4	Create and modify a form	154, 163
W2000E.6.5	Create and modify a form control (e.g., add an item to a drop-down list)	158, 163
W2000E.6.6	Use advanced text alignment features with graphics	207, 208
W2000E.6.7	Customize toolbars	264, 270
W2000E.7	**Collaborating with workgroups**	
W2000E.7.1	Insert comments	187, 191
W2000E.7.2	Protect documents	188, 191
W2000E.7.3	Create multiple versions of a document	182, 191
W2000E.7.4	Track changes to a document	184, 191
W2000E.7.5	Set default file location for workgroup templates	125, 191
W2000E.7.6	Round Trip documents from HTML	238

APPENDIX

B

Glossary

active document a document currently available for editing

add-in a program added to an application for additional functionality, like the Spelling tool

address book an electronic file with names, addresses, and other data on people you contact

align to place text either to the left, center, or right relative to the margins

anchor in desktop publishing, to secure the location of a graphic relative to a character, line, paragraph, or page

application window a container within the Windows interface that displays a program

applications programs that allow you to complete specific tasks, such as word processing

ascending order sorted A to Z, or smallest to largest

AutoCorrect a Word feature that automatically corrects commonly-misspelled words based on entries in a dictionary

AutoFit a Word tables feature that automatically adjusts column width to fit existing text

AutoFormat the Word tool that automatically formats headings, borders, numbered and bulleted lists, and certain symbols

automatic save a feature of Word and other word processing programs that automatically saves a backup copy of active documents for recovery in the event of an unexpected shutdown

autonumbering Word's ability to keep track of and number paragraphs sequentially

AutoText a Word innovation that allows you to store frequently-used text and graphics and quickly insert them into documents

Backspace a keyboard key often represented by a left arrow; when pressed, backspace deletes the character to the left of the insertion point

balance to divide text evenly between columns

block any word or group of consecutive words in a word processing document

boldface   a font style in which printed text is darker than normal for the typeface

bookmark   a word in the text of a document that marks a location to which a user can automatically return without scrolling

border   printable lines around text or cells in a table

browser   an application that allows the user to view Web pages and "surf" the Internet or an intranet

bullet character   a special character, such as a dot or an asterisk, used to identify separate points or items in a list

button   a feature of dialog boxes and toolbars; initiates an action, such as changing formats or closing a dialog box

callout   in desktop publishing, text that describes and points to an area in a graphic

Caps Lock   a key on a computer keyboard that can be toggled on or off to type uppercase or lowercase letters

catalog   a main merge document that allows you to arrange data source records in a list, such as a phone directory

cell   a division of a table; the intersection of a row and a column

center   text alignment that positions text midway between the left and right margins

character map   a Windows feature that shows the letters, numbers, and other symbols available in a font

chart   a visual representation of numeric data

click   the action of pressing the left mouse button to select an object or command

Click and Type   a new feature of Word 2000 that automatically inserts the necessary spacing characters to place the insertion point where you've double-clicked on the page to type text

clip art   in desktop publishing, commercially available graphics and other images you can import into an application and then position, resize, and edit for use in various documents

clipboard an area of memory reserved by Windows for the temporary storage of text and images so they can be moved or copied within or between documents and applications

close to remove a window and its contents (application or document) from the desktop when you are finished working with it; closing does not remove programs or documents from your disks or hard drive

collapse in Outline view, to hide body text and subheadings under other headings to focus on higher-level topics

Collect and Paste new feature in Office 2000 that lets you copy multiple items to the Windows clipboard and paste one, several, or all of them in any order you want

column a vertical division of a page between the margins, or a vertical section in a table

column break a code that can be inserted into a column to indicate the point where text should wrap to the next column

command bar one of the available menu bars or toolbars in an application, used to access the features of a progam

comments "pop-up" notes that can be inserted into documents and viewed during the editing process

context-sensitive features that become available in an application based on what task is being performed

control on forms and in dialog boxes, a control might be represented by a text field or drop-down list; a place where the user can make a choice or enable a feature

Control Panel a Windows 95 program that allows users to customize various Windows settings; the Control Panel is accessed from the Start menu and is located under Settings

convert to change a document so it can be used in an application other than the application in which it was created

copy to create a duplicate of a file, text, or graphics for use elsewhere in the same or another document

crop to cut off unwanted parts of a graphic image

cursor   the flashing line in the document window that indicates where the next character will be inserted (see *insertion point*)

custom dictionary   a list of correctly-spelled words created by the user that were not included in the Microsoft dictionary

customize   to change default settings of an application according to user preferences

cut   to move text or graphics to the clipboard so they can be pasted to another location

data source   the file that contains information broken down into specific fields for use in a merge

database   a collection of information organized into categories for fast and easy retrieval

default   a pre-existing setting for hardware or software the user can choose to accept or change

Delete (Del)   a key on a computer keyboard used to erase unwanted text to the right of the insertion point

demote   to move an item to a lower level of an outline

descending order   sorted Z to A, or largest to smallest

desktop   the control center for Windows

desktop publishing (DTP)   the use of a computer to produce printed material that contains text and graphics

destination application   in OLE, the program into which an object is pasted

dialog box   a window that appears when a Windows-based program requires more information from the user to complete a task

document   a word processing file created by a user

document incompatibility   in mail merging, a condition where Word doesn't recognize either the data source or the main document as a valid merge file

document map   a Word feature that shows all headings in a document so the user can quickly move to any section to edit

document window   the space defined by and contained within an application window where the user enters text to create a document

double-clicking   depressing and releasing the primary mouse button twice in rapid succession without moving the mouse between clicks

drag   to move the mouse while pressing one of the buttons

drag-and-drop   the method for moving or copying selected text or files that requires pressing the mouse button and moving the pointer to the new location before releasing the button

drive   a device used to transfer programs and information such as document files between disk storage and a computer's memory; a computer system may contain several drives, for example, a hard drive, a floppy drive, and a CD-ROM drive

drop cap   in desktop publishing, enlarging the first letter of a paragraph to extend over several lines

drop-down list   options available when a user clicks a downward-pointing arrow on a button

dynamic   an object, field, or cell that is linked to and changes in response to another object, field, or cell

embed   to copy a file created in one application into a document created in a different application

end of document mark   the short horizontal line, visible in Normal view, that marks the point past which you cannot enter text

endnote   a reference that appears in a list (with others) at the end of a document

end-of-section marker   a marker inserted by Word to distinguish the end of a section (such as a change in column layout, header/footers, or orientation) within a document

execute   to launch an application, macro, or other program

expand   in Outline view, to display previously hidden body text and subheadings; to view lower levels of a document's organization

face (typeface)   the design shared by a set of characters

field   a category of information in a database, like first name or address

field names   the names given to various categories of information in a database

file   a collection of data saved on a computer system

fill   a color or pattern inside a drawn object

filter   a program that translates a particular type of file (such as TIFF or EPS graphic images) so the file can be used in a specific application; in a merge, the process of selecting certain records and eliminating others from the merge

Find   a Windows and Word feature that locates files, text strings, formatting, or special codes in a document or folder

first-line indent   an indent applied to the first line of a paragraph

first-line indent marker   a marker displayed on the ruler to indicate that a line is indented

folder   a "container" created for purposes of organizing and storing files and other folders

font   typeface; a complete set of characters within a specific typeface

font style   variations within a font, such as italic or boldface

footer   text or graphics automatically repeated at the bottom of each designated page

footnote   a reference that appears at the bottom of the page

format   broadly, all the elements that define the appearance of a document; to control or change any of these elements; a set of specifications used to save a file, also known as file type; a process for initializing a floppy or hard disk so it can be used to save files

formats   in Date/Time, referring to the style of the date or time (for example, October 24, 1999 vs. 10/24/99)

formula   an equation used in a worksheet or table

frame   a container that holds an object so it can be repositioned on a page

global macro   an automated series of steps that can be run in any documents that share the Normal template

graphics   pictures or images that can be imported into documents

gridlines nonprinting vertical and horizontal lines that designate rows and columns in a table

group to unite two or more selected objects so they are treated as one for purposes of moving and resizing

gutter the white space separating columns of text

gutter margin extra space added to inside margins of a document that will be bound

handles markers that appear around a selected graphic object and are used to resize the object

hanging indent a paragraph formatting style with the first line of a paragraph aligned with the left margin, and subsequent lines indented

hard return a code inserted when the Enter key is pressed to designate a new paragraph

hardware the physical components of the computer system

header text or graphics that are automatically repeated on the top of designated pages

header row in a data source, the top row containing field names

highlight transparent color applied by the user to text for the purpose of emphasis

highlighting contrasting color applied by Word to text or menu options to indicate that the item has been selected

home page the first, typically introductory, page of a Web site

HTML (hypertext markup language) the programming and formatting language of the Web (a native document type for Office 2000)

hyperlink text or object in a document that, upon mouse click, takes the user to another location in the current document, another document, a Web site, or e-mail message

I-beam the form taken by the mouse pointer when it is located within a document window, used to position the insertion point

icons small pictures that represent programs and files used in a graphical user interface

import to bring a file created in one application into another application

indent to move text in from the left or right margins

Insert (Ins) a key on the keyboard that allows toggling between Insert and Overtype modes of text entry

insertion point the place where text will be entered in a word processing document, designated by a flashing vertical line (see *cursor*)

Internet the worldwide series of connected computers, for posting and accessing information about almost any topic imaginable

intranet a company-based internet; a series of connected computers, generally within one company, displaying information by, about, and for the benefit of the company and its employees

italics a font style in which text is slanted to the right

justify a type of alignment in which text is lined up evenly with both the left and right margins (also referred to as *full*)

kerning increase or decrease in the space between characters; expanding or contracting text

keyboard shortcut two or more keys pressed at once to execute a command; for example, Ctrl+Home takes you to the beginning of the active document

landscape a page orientation where text is rotated so it prints parallel to the long side of the paper

launch to start a program

layering placement of objects "on top of" text or other objects in a document, as if the objects were on printed transparency sheets

leader a type of tab that inserts dots or other characters to help the reader follow to the tabbed text

leading (pronounced "ledding") the space above or below one or more lines of text (see *line spacing*)

left indent marker a marker on the ruler that indicates where the left indent is located relative to the left margin

line spacing   the number of lines separating lines of text

link   to connect two files from different applications, such as a Word document and an Excel worksheet

local macro   a macro stored in one particular Word document

locked columns   columns whose widths cannot be adjusted

macro   a set of recorded instructions designed to *play* automatically

main dictionary   a file supplied with Word, containing a list of thousands of words used to check spelling

main document   in merging, the document that contains the field codes and formatted text that will be merged with a data source

margin   the white space around the edges of a document

master document   a collection of subdocuments

maximize   to make a window fill the entire desktop

menu bar   the bar containing lists of options available in a program or window

merge   to combine a data file with a form document to produce mass mailings, labels, and lists

merge cells   a Word tables feature that allows you to combine two or more cells into one

merge field code   a code representing data in a data file; it is replaced with actual data as the result of a merge

minimize   to reduce an application or document window to the size of an icon, allowing it to continue running in the background while another program has priority

mirror margins   margins that are the same on opposite sides of the page for back-to-back printing

module   a section of programming code that plays when you run a macro

mouse   an input device used to activate commands and select text by pointing and clicking

move   to reposition text or objects from one location to another

navigation   the process of moving around in a document, or between linked documents

navigation buttons   controls located on the bottom of a data form used to move to the previous and next records in a data source

new document   a document, just created, that is blank

newspaper columns   segments of text arranged vertically on a page; when text reaches the end of a segment, it wraps to the top of the next segment

nonbreaking (spaces, hyphens)   specially formatted characters that keep the text on either side of the character from breaking across a line

Normal view   a screen display available in Word that does not show margins; allows for maximum width and editing area

Normal.dot   the "normal" template that appears by default when you create new Word documents

Num Lock   the toggle key on a computer keyboard that allows the calculator keypad to be used for numeric entry or insertion point movement

object   anything that can be created in another application and inserted into Word

Office Assistant   Microsoft's friendly and intuitive help interface

OLE (object linking and embedding)   a protocol that allows applications to communicate with one another; used for creating and updating objects

OLE client   an application that can accept OLE objects

OLE server   an application that can create OLE objects

online form   a document designed for use on the Internet or a company intranet sent and processed via e-mail

open   to make available for use, as in a dialog box or document

operating system   software that manages computer resources (such as memory, disk space, processor time, and peripherals) and allows application programs to run; Windows 95 is an operating system

orientation (page) determines whether a page will be printed with text running horizontally or vertically

orphan a first line of a paragraph left alone at the bottom of a page

outline a document structured by topic headings from major topics through minor topics

Outline view a screen display available in Word that shows the structure (headings and titles vs. regular text) of the document

Overtype mode new keystrokes that replace existing text; the opposite of Insert mode

page break a code that indicates the end of a physical page

paginate to insert a page break

paragraph formatting the indents, line spacing, text flow, and tabs related to a paragraph

parallel columns two or more segments of text that are arranged vertically on a page and correspond to each other

password a secret word or code entered by a user to secure a document so it cannot be opened by others

paste to copy text or objects from the clipboard into a document

Paste Special a Word command that allows you to link or embed an object from another application into a Word document

personal computer (PC) a computer, designed for use by an individual, that contains its own central processing unit and memory

picture a piece of art that can be inserted into a Word document

picture bullet a bullet character that is graphical, as opposed to a symbol or other text character

picture placeholders empty boxes that can be inserted into a Word document to represent the eventual placement of graphics

play to run or execute a macro

point a measurement unit used to describe the size of type; 1/72 of an inch

portrait a page orientation in which text is printed parallel to the short side of the paper

Print Layout view a Word screen display that shows the document as it will be printed with headers, footers, and margins

printer font a font available to a printer, but for which there is no matching screen display font

promote to move an item to a higher level in a outline

properties the characteristics of a file, control, or object, such as its format, size, and date modified

protect (a form) to lock a document so a user cannot change the structure of the form

pull quote in desktop publishing, a quote taken from a document, often framed in a box for special emphasis

query a method of retrieving specific information from a database

read-only a setting that allows others to view, but not edit, a document

record in a database, a collection of related items, such as an individual's name, address, and city, within a mailing list

redo a Word tool that restores the previously-undone action

reference mark the number, or other character, that designates a reference supported by a footnote or endnote

repagination a Word feature that automatically reassigns page breaks when text has been entered or deleted

replace an operation that substitutes one text string or formatting type for another

reverse video a display mode in which the background and foreground colors of surrounding text are reversed to highlight text

revert to return to a previously-saved version of a file

right-click an action in which the user clicks the right mouse button; to open a context menu

right indent marker a marker located on the ruler that indicates where the right indent is located relative to the right margin

route to send a document in succession to other users for viewing and editing

row a horizontal group of cells in a table

ruler a Word feature that shows page measurements, left and right margins, tabs, and indents

run to play back a macro

save to copy information from the computer's active memory to permanent storage such as a floppy disk

Save As the command that allows the user to open a dialog box and choose a name and location for a file

scalable a font that can be resized—all TrueType fonts are scalable

screen font a font that is available only for display on a monitor

ScreenTip messages that pop up on screen when the mouse pointer rests on certain areas of the window

scroll bar the horizontal and vertical bars to the right of and below a document window that enable the user to see parts of the document not included in the current screen display

section a portion of a document that includes a page, a column, or some formatting variation

select to designate a text string or an object by clicking or dragging to highlight it; the next operation will affect the selected item

shading gray (or other colored) background tones added to text or table cells

Shortcut bar Microsoft Office's customizable collection of "one-click" shortcuts to launching Office programs and tools

shortcut key a key or a combination of keys that can be pressed in place of using the mouse to initiate an action

shortcut menu the context-sensitive menu that appears when the mouse is right-clicked

Shrink-to-Fit the command available in Print Preview that decreases the size of a slightly-too-large document to fit one page

Shut Down an option on the Windows 95 Start menu that closes all applications and prepares the computer to be turned off or restarted

size/resize to reduce or enlarge a window on the desktop

soft page break a page break inserted automatically when text overflows to the next page

software all the instructions a computer can execute (includes both application programs (like Word) that carry out specific tasks, and operating systems (like Windows 95/98 and 2000) that make the computer's resources available to applications; a computer program)

sort to reorder words, lines, or paragraphs in alphabetical or numerical order

source application in OLE, the program used to create the object

source document a document containing information for one or more records that will be entered into a data source file

spacing the unoccupied area between margins in columns; (see *gutter*)

spell check automatically review the active document for potential spelling errors

spin box a type of control used in a Windows dialog box to increase or decrease numeric values

split to divide a cell in a table into two or more cells; to divide the screen between two or more document windows

spreadsheet a document with data displayed in rows and columns, often containing calculations and formulas (created with programs like Excel and Lotus 1-2-3)

Start menu the menu that appears when the Start button is clicked, which enables the user to access Windows features and applications

static unchanging; the opposite of *dynamic*; (formulas in Word tables are described as static because, once a formula has been entered in a table cell, the result does not change until it is updated, even if the contents of the cells in the column or row change)

status bar the bar at the bottom of a document window that gives information about the current document, such as page number and cursor position

style paragraph and text formatting that is saved so it can be applied to other text

subdocument part of a master document; can be opened and edited separately from the master

symbol any character, available in a font, that is not a letter, numeral, or punctuation mark

tab order on a form, the order in which the controls are activated by tabbing

tab stops measurements on the ruler that indicate where the insertion point will move when the Tab key is pressed

table text that is entered in rows and columns

Taskbar Windows desktop feature that contains the Start button and buttons for any applications currently running

template a pattern for the text, graphics, and formatting of a document

text box a graphic frame that contains text

text effects a Word formatting feature that allows the user to add pizzazz to text by making it sparkle, shimmer, etc.

text string one or more consecutive characters

theme a collection of fonts, backgrounds, colors, and graphics that form the basis for a document or Web page

thesaurus a built-in feature of Word that provides a list of synonyms for a selected word

Tip wizard a Word feature that provides tips to help you learn about the software's many features

title bar the horizontal bar at the top of an application window that displays the name of the application along with the Minimize, Maximize, and Close buttons for the application window

toggle to switch between two options by pressing a key or a toolbar button

tool tip the ScreenTip that appears when you point to a toolbar button; displays the name of the toolbar button

toolbar a bar containing buttons that carry out specific functions, such as saving and printing

track changes   a Word feature that enables the user to see where others have edited a document

typeface (face)   the design shared by a set of characters

underline   an attribute of a font that appears as a line underneath characters

undo   to reverse an action

ungroup   to separate several objects or several parts of one object into smaller, distinct units

unselect   to remove the selection from a text string or object; the action of clicking away from the current selection

variable text   in a main merge document, variable text is the text that changes as information for each record is inserted; merge fields are inserted as placeholders for variable text

version   the content of a file at a given point in time; enables the user to create and save multiple versions of the same document

vertical centering   to position text midway between the top and bottom margins of a page

view   one of several different ways to look at and work in a document, depending on what is being done

virus   malicious code designed to run automatically on a computer

virus detection   software that scans new files for malicious code and attempts to disable it

watermark   an image that remains stationary on the user's screen during scrolling operations

Web Layout view   displays a document as it would appear in a Web browser

Web page   a document prepared and posted on the World Wide Web

Web site   a collection of linked documents posted on the World Wide Web

weight   a characteristic of lines or a typeface based on thickness

widow   the last line of a paragraph at the top of a new page

wildcards   characters that can be used in a Find operation to replace unidentified characters

Windows   Microsoft's graphical user interface/operating system developed to take advantage of faster, more powerful PCs

wizard   a program that walks a user through a series of steps to accomplish a certain task

word processing programs   applications designed to produce text-based documents that are easy to edit, format, and print

WordArt   a program used to create special visual effects with text

wrap   to flow from one line to the next automatically without the user entering a return

zoom   to increase or decrease the size of the text or objects on the display

Index

Note to the Reader: First level entries are in **bold**. Page numbers in **bold** indicate the principal discussion of a topic or the definition of a term. Page numbers in *italic* indicate illustrations.

Microsoft Office User Specialist

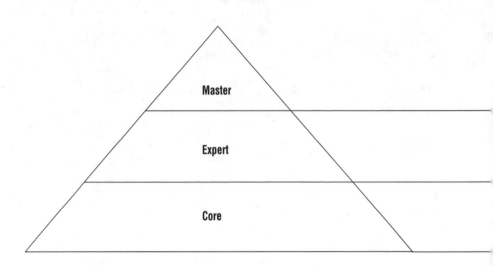

Level	Description	Requirements
Master	Becoming a Microsoft Office User specialist at the Master level indicates that you have a comprehensive understanding of Microsoft Office 2000.	Pass all FIVE of the required exams: Microsoft Word 2000 Expert Microsoft Excel 2000 Expert Microsoft PowerPoint 2000 Microsoft Outlook 2000 Microsoft Access 2000
Expert	Becoming a Microsoft Office User specialist at the Expert level indicates that you have a comprehensive understanding of the advanced features in a specific Microsoft Office 2000 application.	Pass any ONE of the Expert exams: Microsoft Word 2000 Expert Microsoft Excel 2000 Expert
Core	Becoming a Microsoft Office User Specialist at the Core level indicates that you have a comprehensive understanding of the core features in a specific Microsoft Office 2000 application.	Pass any ONE of the Core exams: Microsoft Word 2000 Microsoft Excel 2000 Microsoft PowerPoint 2000 Microsoft Outlook 2000 Microsoft Access 2000